The Bitter End of the British Raj

Ian Smith

The story of an Anglo-Indian boy growing up in India, during the latter stages of the British Raj

Copyright © Ian A C Smith 2016

All rights reserved.
No part of this publication may be reproduced,
stored in a retrieval system or transmitted in any form or by any means
electronic, photocopying, recording, or on the internet, or otherwise
without the prior permission of the copyright holder.

Cover photograph: 'The Taj Mahal at sunset' ID 16505722 © David Evison, Dreamtime.com

Acknowledgements

My heartfelt gratitude to all the selfless folk without whom this book would never have seen the light of day. A special thank you to Nick, my son, and Teresa, my daughter, for providing the initial task of proof-reading and editing and to Carol Warren-Smith, retired teacher and friend, for her final review/critique and invaluable constructive advice.

Others I must not fail to mention are Caroline Beveridge, FIBIS (Families in British India Society) volunteer, researcher and on-line friend, for her relentless efforts in providing vital family historical information and not forgetting Robert Nichols, who carried out further research on my behalf into births, marriages and deaths in the U.K. and overseas. All of these people declined any reward.

I have reserved my last humble thanks to the person who reviewed the initial raw draft of this book and whose words of encouragement inspired me to take this memoir all the way to publication. Thank you very much, Terry Fletcher.

"A most enjoyable pastime. I think you already know that. Your story simply holds the reader spellbound. If, like me, the reader has shared a similar upbringing, then it isn't rocket science for me to forecast that it 'could' be a hit. This story shouldn't go unpublished."

Terry Fletcher, Editor of 'The Anglo-Indian Portal'.

Please Note:

With the many various dialects spoken throughout the Indian subcontinent, those of us born in India, but whose mother tongue was English, invariably communicated with the indigenous population in what would be considered colloquial Urdu, the words and spelling of which, in this book, may not be relied upon to be sufficiently accurate.

Contents

Heritage	1
Early Recollections	8
Off to Boarding School	10
Homecoming	13
Army Life	17
Bad Behaviour	20
Adventure	24
Military Social Life	27
Servants	30
Swimming Lesson	32
What War?	38
Barnes High School	42
Bullyboy	45
All Change	49
Crime and Punishment	53
Snakes and Fagging	56
Mid-term Break	58
Murree	60
White Christmas	65
Back to School	68
Evacuated from School	71
Quetta 1947	74
Fun and Games	77
No. 1 Lytton Road	79

Hard Times	81
The Garden of Eden	85
Grease Monkeys	92
Tribal Life	96
Move Yet Again	101
The Big Move	104
The Bombshell	109
On Our Way to England	112
We've Arrived	116
The Workhouse	118
New School	119
Halfway House	123
Joe and Matt Emmett	125
He's Been Found!	128
Bad Boy	132
Away to Sea	135
Disillusioned	139
A Second Chance	141
Epilogue	145

About the Author

My quest to discover answers to questions posed by my somewhat unusual beginnings have necessitated a process of self-education. My father's efforts to have me educated at a prestigious boarding school in India failed when I was just nine years old. A mysterious inability to grasp the fundamentals of reading and writing severely hampered my academic progress. This may have been the reason for my challenging behaviour and contempt towards authority.

With the abundance of time which retirement provided I seized the opportunity to take advantage of the benefits of the internet, which included on-line tutorials, designed to help those with a less than adequate education. Much effort was needed to acquire the literacy skills which I had lacked throughout my life. The computer which I had bought, prior to retiring, became my saviour and I value it most of all among my humble possessions. Knowledge is now a mere click away.

Attempts to read books always used to end in disappointment and frustration, forcing me to abandon them. However, my effort to self-educate proved slightly more fruitful and I now enjoy a modicum of confidence in expressing myself through my writing. Although I have no knowledge of how a written work should be constructed I hope that, in this book, my effort to relate a series of anecdotes and present them in a prose narrative is acceptable.

My initial intention was to make available to my four children the complexities of their ancestry, in the hope that one day, like me, they may also become interested in their family history. The discovery of many hitherto unknown facts about my forebears and my colonial beginnings gave me great satisfaction and instilled in me a sense of belonging.

This exercise gradually developed into a need to release an inner captive voice. The privacy of my own home provided protection from ridicule and the process gave me the opportunity to indulge in a personal retrospective journey. It also helped me to overcome some of my inner conflicts and rewarded me with endless hours of enjoyment.

Heritage

It was neither by chance, nor quirk of nature, that three generations of my forebears and I were born and raised in India. It was in fact the result of an experiment in genetic engineering, which served the cause of Western imperialism. The results of this experiment became the deciding factor in the race between European nations to secure and dominate the lucrative international trade in exotic commodities such as silk, cotton, tea, spices, indigo, opium and other high-value goods. Other competing nations like the Portuguese, Dutch, French and Danish were content to tolerate inter-racial relationships in order to promote confidence within the indigenous population. The British however, took things a step further.

From the early 17th century, The British East India Trading Company realised that the strict religious caste system among their local employees presented them with a barrier to their ambitious expansion plans. In addition, the Christian missionaries were failing to provide enough of the right quality of converts, because those they had managed to convert were from the illiterate lower classes. Quite simply, it was far easier to convince the low-caste members that they would be redeemed from their lowly status by converting to Christianity.

Further threats to their expansion plans were the devastating effects of tropical heat and endemic disease, which were wreaking havoc on their European employees. The cost and viability of recruiting suitable labour in England, training them and transporting them out to India, only for them to quickly succumb to heatstroke, malaria or dysentery, was questionable. The long-term interests of the company were therefore being jeopardised by a dwindling, unreliable and largely illiterate workforce.

To remedy this, a far-sighted decision was taken by the Company hierarchy, to offer financial inducements to the English officers and soldiers of their protection force to marry Indian women, single European women on the subcontinent being a rarity. Henceforth, a high-value silver coin called a pagoda was awarded to each interracial couple for every child they produced. It was calculated that the offspring of these mixed marriages would produce Christians who would be schooled in the English language and customs. The company would then have an advantage over its competitors by creating a pool of labour that would be obligated to the imperial crown and, it was believed, who would be more resistant to endemic diseases. In short, the Company set about creating a new race, providing them with a cheap, reliable and captive source of labour. Well, I am the product of this crafty bit of genetic engineering. I am in fact a living specimen of the ethnic category called 'Eurasian' – although later, in 1944, at the behest of an eminent lawyer named Frank Anthony, this category was officially renamed 'Anglo-Indian'.

Research into my heritage has revealed that my earliest traceable maternal ancestors to date are James Halfhide and his second eldest son Benjamin Halfhide. James was the owner of Merton Abbey Gate House, Merton, Surrey and lived there from around 1788 to 1804 with his family while running a successful calico printing business, together with his sons. The business operated from buildings situated to the rear of the Gate House and in close proximity to the river Wandle. They imported calico from India through the East India Company, refined it in a bleaching process and printed it with the designs and colours of the day. The end-product was considered to be a luxury fabric, used in the manufacture of soft furnishings. Eventually, in 1804 Halfhide & Sons went bankrupt.

James Halfhide's neighbour during that time was Lord Nelson and it is a documented fact that Nelson purchased a strip of land from my ancestor for the price of £23, in order to extend the grounds of his estate. Later, Charles Smith and his brother, Rear Admiral Isaac Smith, acquired the Merton Abbey Gate House. The latter accompanied Captain Cook aboard the Endeavour and was the first Englishman to set foot on Australian soil. (This information was sourced, courtesy of David Saxby, of The History of London Museum of Archaeology Service and is available at:

http://www.merton.gov.uk/leisure/history-heritage/heritage-sites.html)

In August 1813, Metcalf, an 861 ton ship in the service of the East India Company, arrived in Calcutta from Europe. Among its passengers were Benjamin Halfhide, his wife Elizabeth Halfhide (née Peacock) and their two children, Thomas and Charlotte. At that time Benjamin Halfhide was a Captain in the service of His Majesty's 17th Foot Regiment. In September of the same year, at Fort William, Calcutta, Elizabeth Halfhide gave birth to Robert Sampson Halfhide, who is my maternal great-great-grandfather.

Captain Benjamin Halfhide took part in the Nepal campaign of 1814 - 15, (resulting in the defeat of the poorly-armed and badly-organised people of Nepal), and the 'Aracan' (Burma) campaign of 1824 - 26. In around 1830, Benjamin was raised by purchase to the rank of Brigade Major of the 44th Queen's Foot Regiment at Fort William, Calcutta. By then, he had fathered seven children by his first marriage. In 1831, following the death of his first wife, he married Elizabeth Kinchant, the daughter of a British civil servant, with whom he had two more children.

My maternal grandfather, Frederick James Thomson, was born in Croydon, Surrey in 1888. As a child he attended The White Horse Road Infants' School in Croydon, from June 1892 to March 1896. His poorly-documented and incomplete army service records indicate that he attended The Bishop Whitgift Grammar School in Croydon and then studied at the Central Polytechnic in London. According to those same army records, prior to arriving in India he had worked in British West Africa and had been employed as an executive engineer on several civil engineering projects for the British Government in Nigeria, Sierra Leone and The Gambia.

The precise time of his arrival in India is still the subject of ongoing enquiry, though his marriage to Clarice Margaret Halfhide (my maternal grandmother) is confirmed in their marriage certificate as October 11th 1913 at St Andrew's Church, Darjeeling, West Bengal. Thacker's Directory has an entry which confirms that he was then working for The Amalgamated Tea Companies in Darjeeling as an engineer, from about 1918 until 1920. Subsequently family hearsay has it that he also worked on civil engineering projects for the Indian Government. In 1940 he joined the Army and was immediately given an emergency commission as Captain in the Royal Army Ordinance Corps. In 1946 he resigned his commission and returned to England. His death is recorded as occurring in Wimbledon, in March 1956 at the age of 67.

My earliest traceable ancestor on my father's side is my great-grandfather, Conductor George Smith, whose birth was recorded in 1846 in Bexley, Kent and his death in 1888, in Mandalay, Burma. Initially a Sergeant in the 7/20 or G Battery Royal Artillery, he arrived in India with his regiment sometime around 1870. In 1875, at the age of 29, he transferred to the Indian Ordnance Department where he held the appointment of Sub-Conductor, (later to be promoted to Conductor) and married Elizabeth Jane Huntley in the same year. The marriage took place in Trimulgherry, Andhra Pradesh, India. The couple produced four children, among them my paternal grandfather George Frederick Smith, born in 1881 at Cannanore, Kerala.

In 1907 George married Daisy Constance Pearce in Ferozepur, India. Daisy had been born in Saharanpur, India in 1888 and was only 19 years of age on her wedding day. George was a Guard with the North Western Railway and was seven years older than his bride. Their only child, my father, George Lindsay Smith was not born until six years later in 1913, also in Ferozepur. George Frederick died in Lahore in 1915, when my father was just two years old.

Daisy's father was Robert Burns Pearce, who was born on May 12th, 1858 in Rochester, Kent, England. He married Jane Lindsay Smith on November 23rd 1880 in Delhi, India. Jane Lindsay's father is named on the marriage certificate as William Lindsay Smith. Legend has it that William took part in the 2nd Afghan Campaign from 1878 to 1880; he was a Corporal in the 2023 92nd foot, regiment and suffered severe wounds during battle. He was repatriated to his home town of Arbroath in Scotland, where he later died from the effects of the wounds. No mention is made of Jane Lindsay's mother nor was there any evidence of her during several years of research into family history records. Jane's photograph would indicate that she was of mixed race and therefore she would certainly have been the lady that had a distinct bearing on my claim to Anglo-Indian heritage.

George Lindsay Smith and my mother, Marion Edith Thomson, were married in 1936, in Moradabad, India; he was 23 and my mother was 16 at the time. She had been born in Darjeeling, West Bengal and died in Scartho Road Hospital, Grimsby, in 1978. My father worked for the North Western Railway, just as his father had done, but then he enlisted in the British Army in 1941. He died in The Whittington Hospital, Archway, North London in 1967.

I was born in February 1938, towards the end of the era of British Empire rule in India, the so-called 'Raj' period. To add some perspective, it was also the year before the invasion of Poland by Nazi Germany. My birthplace is a town called Moradabad, which is in the state of Uttar Pradesh, situated about 104 miles, or 167 km east of the capital city of New Delhi. The town was established in 1600 by Prince Murad, the eldest son of the Mogul Emperor Shah Jahan. Moradabad passed into British hands in about 1801 and was designated a British Army garrison town. At the time of my birth, the North Western Railways employed my father and step-grandfather; Father was a guard and Grandfather was a mail train driver. These were considered to be well-paid jobs at the time. An old family photograph, taken around 1940, confirms that the family lived in a large house with a mock Roman façade. A major road separated the house from the railway station. I remember the clouds of black smoke that could be seen and the piercing sound of the steam whistles that could be heard above the din of daily life, as trains entered and left the station.

We lived in an extended family unit: Nana and Papa, Father and Mother, Theo,

Barbara and me. In the house next door lived relatives on my father's side: the Skilling family – comprising my grandmother's sister, Aunty Doris, husband Malcolm and their children. Mutual visits would take place on a daily basis. Auntie Doris and my grandmother were members of the Pearce family, the male lineage of which was English, having been traced back to John Pearce, who was born in 1745, in the village of Hoo, near Rochester, Kent. The family property was called Blue Bell Hill Farm, which I understand is still a working farm today.

Theo 4, Barbara 1, Ian 3

As a child, I can remember my grandmother often referring to a Baronet William Pearce and claiming that she was closely related to him, the significance of which I never quite understood at the time. However, I mentioned this to my wife Isabel a few times, after I had retired; she encouraged me to begin investigating my family history. So it was, with Baronet William Pearce, that my interest in family history was awakened. By chance I discovered that my second cousin, by the name of Lesley Pearce, lived quite close by to me and we made arrangements to meet up. He told me that he had already completed an extensive research of the Pearce family lineage and gave me a copy of the family history. He then explained that we could both claim a direct blood relationship to Sir William Pearce as, his father, Bertram Pearce and my grandmother, Daisy Constance Pearce, were distant cousins to Sir William Pearce. My grandmother, it seemed, had been right all along.

William Pearce was born in 1833 in Brompton, Kent and apprenticed at Chatham dockyard, where he studied naval architecture. He superintended the building of HMS Achilles, the first iron-clad ship built in a royal dockyard. The ship was completed in 1861. He went on to serve with Robert Napier and Son as General Manager and later was to become Chairman of the Fairfield Shipbuilding and Engineering Company Shipyard in Govan, Glasgow; this was then renowned as the leading shipbuilding company in the world. At a later date he assumed total proprietorship of the shipyard. William also served for ten years as Conservative Member of Parliament for the Govan Division, Lanarkshire and was created Baronet in 1887.

He died in 1888 in London and his estate was declared at £1,069,669. During his working life he had been responsible for the building of ships for the Cunard Line, The P&O Shipping Company, The New Zealand Shipping Company and the Nile Fleet, as well as many other ships for the Royal Navy. After his death his wife bequeathed the Mitchell Library and the Pearce Institute to the city of Glasgow, for the enjoyment and leisure of the shipyard workers. The Blue Riband Prize, awarded for the fastest crossing of the Atlantic by a passenger-carrying liner, was instituted by Sir William Pearce. On his death, the people of Glasgow petitioned to have him buried in the city but family considerations overruled and he was buried at his place of birth in Gillingham, Kent. However, the grateful Glaswegians honoured him by having a statue in his image erected in Govan Cross, where it still stands today, opposite the Pearce Institute.

His only son, Sir William George Pearce, second Baronet inherited his father's title and his fortune. On his death in 1907 he was interred at St Mary's Church, Chilton Foliat, near Hungerford, Berkshire, about twenty miles from where I now live. Three weeks after his death his widow, Caroline Eva Pearce (née Coot), also died. The family fortune, estimated to be in excess of £1,000,000, was bequeathed to Trinity College, Cambridge. It is said to be the largest single donation ever received by the College from a single benefactor. This information was sourced from the Mitchell Library.

Baronet Sir William Pearce - in George Square, Glasgow

Early Recollections

My earliest memory is of an incident that occurred when I was a little over two years old. It concerns the vivid image of a portly Indian man dressed in white, with his head swathed in a white *pagree* (a traditional Indian headdress), with a fancy fan shape on one side. He was saying something to me as I was making my way towards him, or rather towards what may have been the greater attraction, the large object next to him; I later learnt that this was a car, which had been hired to take the family to church for my sister Barbara's christening.

The man suddenly ran forward, grabbing hold of me and picking me up. He began to shout very loudly, so loud that I remember getting quite upset. Through my tears I could see other men running towards us. The *pagree* man kept shouting and trying to console me at the same time. Then, as if from nowhere, my mother and other members of my family appeared and the man handed me to my mother. Everybody seemed to be looking in the direction of some bushes and shrubs. Suddenly they all started to cheer and laugh and I could see two men walking towards us holding aloft, on crossed sticks, a long black object.

It was not until I was a bit older and the family were sitting on the veranda one evening, entertaining some friends, when Nana began relating this incident to them. I immediately pricked up my ears and clearly recalled the images of that day. It was then I learnt that I had apparently disturbed a cobra, while toddling through one of the flowerbeds. Nana declared that I had probably cheated certain death that day. The man turned out to be the chauffeur of the hired car and he told Nana that I had passed within a few feet of the cobra. It has always puzzled me why this incident should have left such a lasting impression on me.

Other trivial but indelible memories (and some not so trivial but equally indelible) began forming as I grew a little older: the excitement of riding in the front seat of a *tonga* and being allowed to sit beside the driver and watching the flight of flying foxes (fruit bats) as dusk fell. The latter had been roosting all day in a large mango tree, which overhung the servants' quarters; being covered in multi-coloured dyes by people celebrating the Hindu festival of Holi. I can still visualise with surprising clarity these meaningless little events in my early life.

Another vivid memory is the barber's daily visit, which was a source of amusement to me. I loved watching him shave Papa with a cut-throat razor and he would always call me over to dab my nose with shaving soap, saying it was ice-cream, then encourage me to try and lick it off. I hated having to have my hair cut by him, however. His hand-operated clippers pulled and made me wince as they trimmed the hair on the back of my neck. The barber had the most comical way of mounting his bicycle and I always felt compelled to watch him as he left the house. He had fitted extended spindles to either side of the rear wheel axle and, for my amusement, he would place a foot on one of the spindles before launching the bike. Once it was in motion he would jump forward into the air and land on the saddle, then look back at me with a big grin on his face. The devilish anticipation of him missing the saddle and falling off never failed to amuse me.

Off to Boarding School

Interaction between parents and their children, for many of the so-called 'Children of the Raj', was somewhat restricted, due mainly to the practice of most domiciled Europeans and Anglo-Indians of choosing to employ domestic servants. The *ayah* (woman servant, or nanny) was tasked with the care of the younger children from infancy up to school-age and in some cases even longer. The bond between *ayah* and child sometimes became stronger than that of the natural mother with her offspring. I recall the reassuring smile of my *ayah*, Lavinia, the shiny jewel that adorned the left side of her nose and her soft voice singing me to sleep with the same repetitive Indian lullaby. I still remember the tune and the Urdu words and I often sang it to my granddaughter, Christina, when she was a baby. She loved it and would sometimes ask me to sing it to her, even when she was much older.

Another reason for lack of parent-child interaction was the almost universal practice of sending children to boarding school, where they spent the best part of the year away from family life. This could be at a very early age and, in my own case, I was just four years old when I was sent away. In early spring 1942, Brother Theo, our cherished teddy bear and I were packed off to Dumbarney Preparatory Boarding School. I still have the photograph of all three of us, which was taken on that day to mark the event. Dumbarney, situated in Mussoorie in the foothills of the Himalayas, was for children whose parents were employed by the railways. Sadly, I have few if any pleasant memories of that school. I remember sleeping in a dormitory of about eight or ten little boys and girls. Matron, whose looks would kill a bull elephant at a hundred yards, would pull me out of bed in the morning and shout in my ear, "You've done it again, haven't you?" She would then pull the bed apart, tugging at the wet sheet, screaming, "Get those wet clothes off, you lazy child!" I was then made to sit in a bowl of water, while she draped my wet sheets and pyjamas over a large inverted cone-shaped wicker construction. This had been placed in the middle of the dormitory, with a *charag* (a small charcoal burner) under it to dry laundry. The mattress was left to air-dry although I don't think it ever dried fully. Matron would dictate prayers each night as we knelt beside our beds, then walk over to me with her index finger pointing upwards saying, "What must you ask Jesus for tonight?"

The regime in the classroom was no more genial than in the dormitory. The teacher was a woman whose looks and manner were not dissimilar to Matron and whose teaching methods were more appropriate to training circus animals. She seemed to spend the whole day screaming like a demented witch! It was she who was responsible for the demise of our teddy bear, grabbing him from me in a fit of temper and tearing one of his arms off. Although she said he would be mended and returned, I never saw poor Teddy again. Looking back, I am convinced that these two women must have graduated from the 'Genghis Khan Academy of Charm' - there were so many sad, tear-stained faces among the other children at that school....

The temperature at this high-altitude school could drop quite low in early spring and late autumn. I don't recall seeing anything resembling a heating system but I do remember that baths were taken in a room attached to the dormitory. The bathroom had a terracotta-tiled floor with a large, galvanised metal tub placed in one corner. Every once in a while I would find myself standing in the bath, along with one or two other children. Supervised by an Indian lady we would take turns to pour the water over ourselves using a large enamel mug and rub our bodies down with a bar of strong smelling soap, then rinse off. A towel would then be thrown over our shoulders and we were encouraged to dry ourselves. I can remember standing there, shivering in the cold and our teeth chattering. At the end of term, when parents arrived to collect their children, they found that many of us were suffering from scab-encrusted chilblains on our ears, noses and knuckles. I'm happy to say that we were never sent back to that school as, by then, my father had left the railway and had enlisted in the British Army.

My personal opinion is that some of these schools were a convenient place for parents to abandon their children out of the way, for the best part of the year. The cooler climate, British education, regimental regime and Christian ethos of these boarding schools made them popular and they were considered superior by most European and Eurasian families. The 1901 census recorded almost three million Europeans living and working on the subcontinent and the so-called 'Hill Schools' were the answer to that demand during the 19th and early 20th century. The majority of these schools were founded by religious organisations. Others, like the Lawrence Colleges, founded by Sir Henry Montague Lawrence in 1847, were initially intended to cater for the large number of orphans created by the high mortality rate of British Army personnel.

Ian 4, Theo 5 & Ted
The day we were sent to boarding school

Homecoming

Back in Moradabad, we were excited to be reunited with the family. Auntie Doris always greeted me by sinking her teeth into my cheek and saying, "I love those dimples," and I would wriggle away and wipe my cheek with the back of my hand. I don't remember any other children of our age living in our neighbourhood but there were quite a few adults. The younger females from the Skilling family next door, delighted in teasing me about my dimples and saying, "Auntie Doris is going to bite them off one day!"

The servants also greeted us enthusiastically; our *ayah* Lavinia, houseboy Premhassi and Bansi the cook all seemed so pleased to see us and made a big fuss of us. When the excitement died down we settled back into family life and began getting used to familiar faces again. Life was so much better at home than at school.

Father's duties kept him away from home for much of the time, as did my grandfather's. However, when Father was around, I tended to avoid his company. He was a man of slim build and stood six feet tall, with dark hair, combed straight back, a sharp nose, a pencil moustache, piercing green eyes and a foul temper. At times his looks would be enough to turn milk sour! He always seemed to be ticking me off whenever he laid eyes on me, or at least, that's how it seemed to me.

Father, George Lindsay Smith. Mother, Marion Edith Smith (nee Thomson)

My mother was small, with well-balanced features, dark hair and a soft voice. A placid soul, she rarely raised her voice to us but, even when she did, it seemed to lack any meaningful authority and was always accompanied by the well-worn phrase, "You wait till your father comes home." This always made me think twice. Mum mostly left the *ayah* to deal with we children, while she went about the business of organising other things in the home.

7 members of the Thomson family in Darjeeling Mum back row second right, about 1933

Nana was a slender-built lady, with long, sand-coloured hair that reached halfway down her back. She could frequently be seen brushing it and then winding it around and coiling it into a bun at the back of her head, where it was kept in place with hairpins. She had an engaging smile and a jovial and sympathetic nature. She took more of an interest in us children, often telling us stories, singing amusing little ditties and dispensing pearls of wisdom. However, most of the time, Theo and I were left to amuse ourselves.

I mentioned earlier that my natural paternal grandfather died when my father was just two years old, which left my grandmother and my father unsupported. Her close relatives were sympathetic and took care of both of them until my father reached school-age. Nana then went into service for a Major Hackett, of the Green Jacket Regiment and his wife. She was governess to their two young children and travelled with the family to Mesopotamia, where the Major had been posted. This employment enabled her to afford the fees to send my father to boarding school, although she still had to rely on relatives to look after him during the school holidays. There were stories of my father being ill-treated by Nana's older brother, Bertie Pearce, with whom he occasionally stayed. Father was educated at The Lawrence College, a boarding school at Ghora Gali, situated in the Murree hills, north of Rawalpindi. Later on, Nana married George MacMullen and they settled back in Moradabad.

We children always called George MacMullen 'Papa'. Papa was a very reserved character. My recollection of him is of a large man, standing very tall, with a mop of snow-white hair and, due to him being a heavy smoker, a bushy, nicotine-stained moustache. He was of Irish decent and was educated in a Catholic Don Bosco orphanage. He once told me that the punishments handed out there were very harsh. Seldom did he show any emotion and he was a tolerant person, very rarely interfering with the way things were run in the family. Off-duty he could often be seen sitting in what he called his 'easy chair' on the veranda, reading the newspaper or filling in the crossword puzzle.

Papa, George Stuart MacMullen. Nana, Daisy Constance McMullen (née) Pearce. Jane Lindsay Pearce (née) Smith - my great grandmother

My idea of fun was when Papa would decide to give his tiger-skins an airing. They would be taken from their storage trunks and laid out on *charpoys* (a simple, Indian rustic bed), the smell of naphthalene filling the air. Papa was a very keen *shakari* (big-game hunter) and he always spent his annual one-month leave on hunting trips in the Shivalik and Kumaon jungles of northern India. Later on in life my father told me that Papa used to organise hunting parties and was on first-name terms with Jim Corbett, the celebrated game warden of the Corbett Game Reserve. He also said that Papa was one of the very few men in India to have been granted a licence to kill four tigers a year. This may seem obscene in this day and age but then it was regarded as some kind of honour, although I doubt very much that he ever achieved his quota! I think the licence may have included tigers shot by other paying members who had been invited along with him.

Prior to these hunting trips, the real fun would begin. The guns and fishing tackle would be brought out, along with the cleaning materials. I couldn't wait for the gun cases to be opened and to feast my eyes on those beautiful shotguns and rifles. The shotgun barrels would be cleaned and oiled with rods and bunting but the rifles had to be cleaned with a 'pull-through'. This was a strong cord which, on one end, had a narrow cylindrical brass weight attached and at the other a loop into which was threaded a piece of '3-in-1' oiled bunting or a cylindrical stiff brush. Papa would remove the bolt, feed the end of the long brass weight into the breech, allowing it to travel down the barrel, and I would catch it at the muzzle end. With encouraging words from Papa, I would pull the cord through the barrel, while he held on tight to the rifle. I can still smell the '3-in-1' oil and see the smile on his face as I was tugging the cord.

Papa also taught me the names of the component parts of guns and how to disassemble and assemble them. Looking back, I think these little episodes must have been my first enjoyable learning experience. Papa spoke in his usual soft, relaxed voice, while holding the rifle obliquely across his chest. He began naming the various components, starting with the stock and then moving to the working parts: the breech, bolt, trigger, trigger-guard, safety catch, rear sight, fore sight and the muzzle.

He then went on to explain how the weapon was armed. Seated in his chair on the veranda, with the rifle to his right shoulder, supporting it with his left hand, then using the index finger and thumb of his right hand, he would say, "You lift the bolt up here and pull it back. The round goes in the breech; you push the bolt forward and the shell gets pushed into the combustion chamber. The bolt is then locked down. When the trigger is pulled, the bullet gets fired out from the muzzle." I don't remember saying anything, but I must have being paying serious attention, as that explanation and demonstration is etched on my brain. Whenever I have had the occasion to handle a firearm, I am reminded of Papa and his guns.

Army Life

When I was five years old life began to get a little more interesting. I vividly remember a train journey involving the whole family, as well as the servants. Along a crowded and chaotic railway platform we followed some *coolies* (porters) who carried our belongings on their heads - large black tin trunks and huge bedding rolls. Finally, we arrived at what my father said was our carriage. As we waited to board a fierce argument erupted between my father and some Indian people, who were already occupying the carriage. My father was insisting that they vacate immediately, arguing that he had reserved it for his family. Nana suggested that we share the carriage but I remember him turning to Nana and saying, "I'm not having my family share with those filthy bastards." His face was red with rage.

An official-looking man, dressed in a white suit and *solar topee* (pith-hat) hurried towards us. Nana said he was the Station Master and he seemed to know my father. He boarded the carriage and quite forcefully ejected the Indian family. Items of their luggage were being thrown from the doors, landing on the platform with a thud and a cloud of dust. Once things had settled down, we boarded the train. The servants made sure that the bedrolls and hand-luggage were in place before making their way to the back of the train, where they would make themselves comfortable in the luggage van, along with the bulk of our belongings. This was where they would spend the rest of the journey.

Throughout the journey, whenever we stopped at stations my father visited the servants and took them some food and drink. This must have been regarded as luxury travel by them, compared to many of their fellow passengers who were obliged to ride on the roof of the train or hang on to the outer handrails of the carriage doors. If any of them tried to hold onto our carriage handrails, my father would threaten to push them off when the train was in motion.

Theo and I frequently stuck our heads out of the window when we realised that the train was approaching a sharp bend. That way we could get a better view of the engine. Our faces became covered in soot and coal dust and our eyes were sore. The heavy smell of burning steam-coal lingered in my nostrils for ages. Nana kept handy a damp flannel and would call us over periodically to have our faces wiped clean. When the train stopped at stations along the way, we listened out for the various station vendors calling out in their sing-song voices, *"Chai garm, garm chai,"* and *"Thandaa pani, thandaa pani."* I had great fun poking my head out of the window and mimicking them. Food was delivered to our carriage by a bearer, dressed in a white, starched uniform. These meals would have had to be ordered in advance by telegraph before the journey began. When the meal was finished the trays, crockery and cutlery would then be collected at the next main stop along the line.

The journey ended at a place called Meerut. As the train slowly entered the station, a number of *coolies*, dressed in their distinctive uniform of red shirts with brass identity plates fastened to their upper arm, ran alongside our carriage until the train came to a stop. They pushed and shoved each other in an excited manner, calling out in an attempt to catch my father's attention, hoping he would select them to carry our luggage. Once the train had stopped he selected a couple of them and noted their arm-band numbers. He then explained how many items of luggage we had and, after a bit of brow beating and haggling, agreed a price.

As we came out of the station building, a stampede of *tongas* (horse-drawn taxis, unique to India) raced towards us, reminiscent of the start of a Roman chariot race, their handlers screaming to attract our attention. After yet another round of selection and haggling, two or three were engaged to transport us and all our luggage to what was to become our new home - for a while at least!

These long, arduous but always exciting rail journeys were to become a feature in our lives, each journey being an adventure in itself. Many schools were tucked away in hill stations, where the climate was much cooler and, as most of the British Army's garrison towns and depots were situated in the red-hot plains, rail travel was the only way to make such long journeys, some taking several days to complete.

At times, stopovers at rail junctions were necessary in order to make connections to final destinations. The train carriages were designed for long-haul and were equipped with drop-down sleeping berths. This vast, British-built rail system, which was originally designed to transport troops and military equipment, was perhaps the most enduring legacy to the Indian nation after the British left India.

British Military Hospital Meerut Cantonment, about 1944 Father, far right in the second row

Meerut was said to be one of the hottest British garrison postings and was also one of the few towns in India not built on a river. It featured prominently during the 1857-8 Indian Mutiny. Our living quarters here were part of a line of about eight or ten uniformly-built bungalows, raised above ground level and built in a kind of rustic colonial style. They were designed to accommodate the families of serving soldiers and were named Gillespie Barracks Married Quarters. A raised tarmac road, with monsoon ditches on either side, separated the Quarters from the BMH (British Military Hospital). On the far side and beyond the BMH, was a prisoner of war camp. It held hundreds of Italian POWs and was run on similar lines to that of an open prison.

One end of our road was a dead end but the other end intersected with a main road. A Gurkha regiment guard room was strategically placed near the intersection, where immaculately turned-out sentries stood on duty around the clock. I would watch them intently while they were being drilled and would then go home and try to imitate them. Using a length of bamboo as my rifle, I would march up and down the veranda shouting orders to myself. On one occasion I was practising my army drill, unaware that some Gurkha soldiers were watching me from the hospital compound across the road. I stopped as soon as I noticed I was being watched and they began to laugh and applaud me. I threw the bamboo down and ran indoors, drenched with embarrassment.

Bad Behaviour

Soon we made friends with a few of the other kids on the camp. There were Sergeant Wilson's two boys whose first names I have completely forgotten, but there was another boy who was quite a bit older than me, whose name I'm not likely to forget: Johnny Eastoe. Johnny was a kind of devil-may-care type and I was told to avoid his company. Nana said that he wasn't the kind of boy that I should be friendly with, as he had been brought up badly. Rumour had it that Johnny's father was permanently absent and his mother didn't enjoy the best reputation within the army community. But I was intrigued by his wayward antics; in fact I envied his Huckleberry Finn reputation and, despite warnings not to form an association with him, I welcomed every clandestine opportunity to do so.

It was now 1943, Papa had retired from the railway before we moved to Meerut and the family had settled into army life. There were, by now, five children: Theo, myself, Barbara, Deanna and Kenneth.

Because he worked in the hospital across the road, we began to see and hear more of my father. The Army seemed to have made him very keen on discipline and hygiene and consequently he imposed a military regime in the home. Strict obedience, time-keeping and impeccable table manners were to be observed. Theo and I were to become less dependent on the *ayah* and more responsible for keeping ourselves clean and tidy. Daily inspections were carried out and from time to time, if fault were found, Father would punish us by making us stand in a corner of one of the rooms, facing the wall. This could last from one hour to a whole day, depending on the severity of the misdemeanour. Extra time would be added if he caught us leaning against the wall during that time!

After a few chance meetings with Johnny Eastoe his relaxed attitude began to rub off on me. I became a little bolder and decided that the Wilson boys' company was too dull. Their father was a Sergeant, and also a strict disciplinarian, and I felt that the boys' spirit of adventure had been knocked out of them.

I began to find the forbidden company of Johnny Eastoe far more exciting. He said and did all the things that I wanted to say and do. He taught me how to make a catapult and showed me all his favourite hiding places. One day he told me that he knew where there was a big lake where we could go fishing and swimming. My confidence grew as he tutored me on how to deal with grown-ups. "Just tell them to go to hell," he would keep saying and, although I could never muster the courage to do so, just the thought of it ignited a spark of power in me!

As my behaviour became more challenging, my father could see that standing me in a corner of a room was becoming much too tame and began to use what he called a 'swish', which was a green branch taken from a neem tree. Once the leaves were removed it formed a perfect cane. The effects would leave purple weals on my legs and backside and Nana would smear them lightly with Germolene ointment to ease the stinging and prevent any infection. She also saved me from many a hiding by humouring my father. On those occasions, as an alternative, he would lock me up in the 'go-down'. 'Go-down' is an anglicised version of the Hindi word meaning storeroom or warehouse – a *godam*. For me it meant the woodshed, which was also used for the storage of miscellaneous, redundant household items. These punishments could last all day and, on a couple of occasions, late into the evening.

Being locked up in the 'go-down' was something I dreaded. I think I may even have preferred a hiding. I always had an intense fear of the dark but being locked up in this way had the added fear of creepy gecko lizards and the real possibility of snakes, scorpions, centipedes and tarantulas, which may have already taken up residence in the wood-pile. Besides, the threat of any one of these creatures entering through the gap under the door while I was in there kept me in a state of constant suspense. The slightest sound or movement would strike terror in me. My imagination would begin to run riot and on occasions, when being confined for long periods, I would lose control of my bodily functions and have to relieve myself on the floor. The first ten minutes or so were usually the worst; after that my eyes would get used to the dark and only then would some of the fear begin to ease.

I screamed myself hoarse on more than one occasion, in a futile attempt to conquer the fear. Nana would sometimes stand outside for a while, trying to calm me down. She would wait until the crying eased and utter words of encouragement, then leave. I would then get up onto one of the tin trunks that were stored there and try to keep one eye on the wood-pile and the other on the gap at the bottom of the door. Nana would sometimes slide a slice of bread wrapped in newspaper through the gap at the bottom of the door. When I was eventually let out it was always Nana who came to release me. She would then make me apologise to my father for my misbehaviour.

Another time, Father tied me to the gatepost for half a day and told all the neighbourhood kids to collect grass to put in front of me, the way you would when feeding an animal. That was because I had failed to wash behind my ears that morning. Father said, "Only animals don't wash." As a punishment for wetting the bed I would be made to stand on a chair on the veranda with a chamber pot on my head. I could hear the laughter coming from passers-by and from the neighbourhood kids. They found it highly amusing; needless to say, I did not!

One evening, when I had turned up late for dinner, he locked me out of the house and ordered the servants not to let me in after they finished their work that night. At first I thought he was just trying to scare me. It was not until the servants had all gone, and the lights started to go off at the hospital across the road and in the neighbouring houses, that it dawned on me that he was serious.

Initially, I just sat on one of the chairs on the veranda listening to the crickets and bullfrogs; but again, I started to think about the lizards, tarantulas, scorpions and all the other creepy-crawlies. Suddenly, the call of a scavenging jackal rang out and panic set in. As the howls seemed to get nearer and nearer, I took up a position at Nana and Papa's window and knocked lightly on it, but there was no answer. I waited for what I thought was ages before trying Nana's window again; still no answer. As I was about to resign myself to spending the night on the veranda, the curtain moved and Nana's face appeared at her window, her index finger placed on her lips indicating silence. I quickly made my way to the front door and waited for her to let me in. I was careful not to be late for a meal again.

Theo and Barbara occasionally got their share as well but, as far as I can remember, they were never locked in the 'go-down'. Father was more lenient with them, only smacking them, or perhaps threatening to use his belt. I by contrast, received many punishments and beatings. Some of these were for what I thought were very minor misdemeanours - such as being a bit cheeky or answering back.

I have long since forgotten most of the incidents that attracted my father's discipline but there were one or two memorable ones. There was one occasion when I told Premhassi that I was allowed to go with him to the bazaar to fetch a watermelon, in spite of my mother having told me that I was not to go. The watermelon became too heavy for Premhassi to carry so we had to roll it back home with our feet. It began to split and the juice covered my shoes and legs. That gave the game away when I got home!

There was also the time I grabbed hold of a curtain to use as a swing, resulting in it coming down, bringing large chunks of cement and plaster off the wall with it. I think I tried fibbing my way out of trouble but Nana probably saved me, as usual. One day, while playing 'horses' with Barbara, I drank water like a horse would, from an earthenware container outside the next-door neighbour's kitchen. I didn't know it was used to wash their baby's nappies in, did I? Then another time, I threw a stone at a neighbour's gander, which had several newly-hatched goslings. The stone missed the gander but fatally struck one of the goslings! Worse still, the geese belonged to one of the officer's wives. She was very upset…

Having said all that, the harsh disciplining of children was not uncommon among the European and Anglo-Indian communities. It would be very difficult for anyone in this day and age to understand why anybody would choose to treat their children so harshly but, in my opinion, parents of that time were obliged to maintain very high standards of family discipline. This was in order to demonstrate to the wider community the preparation of their offspring for their place in the British Empire. It was believed that this overt behaviour would promote their social standing and secure not only their own but their children's economic prospects. As they saw it, a well-mannered, impeccably-behaved, obedient child would be an asset to their parents and to the world. After all, the unforgiving, judgemental Victorian ethos cultivated by the Imperial rulers was reinforced at every level.

As I mentioned earlier, the ancestry of most of the European and Anglo-Indian population in India emanated from the establishment of the East India Trading Company, back in 1600. There followed the continued occupation of the sub-continent by the British and its military might, right up until 1947. After the Sepoy rebellion in 1857, the so-called 'Raj' period was established. This era brought with it a mixture of Victorian and military values, with subordinates and underlings, at whatever level, obliged to grovel to their superiors. I have a copy of a letter, handwritten in 1943 by an ancestor of mine, pleading with the then-Viceroy of India, Lord Lillingworth, to give his son a job on the Railway. Its grovelling, subservient tone would doubtless astonish a present-day reader.

Adventure

As Johnny Eastoe was passing by the house one day, he called out, "Coming fishing?" Fishing! This was something I had never done. In order not to attract the attention of anyone in the house by calling out, I slowly shook my head and then waited for him to pass by. The temptation of adventure became too strong to pass up. Sticking my 'catty' (catapult) in my pocket, I left the house from the back door but kept looking back to make sure nobody saw me. I caught up with him two houses down the road. "Changed your mind then?" he said. "Yeah," I said. I thought it best not to mention that my parents had forbidden me to associate with him.

We crossed over onto the hospital side of the road and dropped down into the monsoon ditch. This way we could avoid being seen by anyone from the married quarters. Once we got to the junction with the main road Johnny said that we would have to cross without being seen by the sentries at the Gurkha guardroom. He said that if they saw us they would take our names and tell our parents. When we got level with the guardroom his plan was to fire a shot with his 'catty' at the red fire buckets that hung on its side wall. This would distract the sentry's attention he said, then I was to make a dash over the main road and drop into the ditch on the other side. I would have to do the same for him when I got there.

The first part worked well; he quickly popped his head above the top of the ditch and loosed off a shot. I heard a dull thud. He must have missed the buckets and hit the wooden guardroom wall. He waited for a second then said, "Go on!" I didn't hesitate. I jumped out of the ditch and, without looking back, dashed across the main road and dropped into the ditch on the other side. I paused for a while; my heart was thumping and I could hear voices coming from the guardroom. It was now my turn to carry out the second part of the plan. This was the first big, independent decision I had had to make in my life and panic and confusion gripped me. Johnny and I were now separated by the main road and unable to communicate.

I knew I would have to do something soon; Johnny was relying on me. I began to claw my way up the side of the ditch to see what was going on. As I raised my head above the line of the road, I could see two Gurkha soldiers having a conversation. I seized the opportunity. Kneeling on one knee, I loaded my 'catty' and aimed at the side wall of the guardroom. The thud on the wall would be the signal for Johnny to cross the road. However, my effort proved to be feeble, as I was further away than Johnny had been for his shot. I didn't have the power or the accuracy to reach the target and my shot landed in the dust, just short and to the side of the two soldiers. Immediately, they spotted me and, for a moment, I froze. One of them headed towards me and, in my effort to get away, I quickly turned towards the ditch, lost my footing and rolled down to the bottom.

As I looked up, the soldier was saying something to me in Hindi that I didn't understand. He then picked me up and ushered me to the guardroom, where I was made to wait outside until the Guard Commander could deal with me. The fearsome-looking Commander came out and asked for my name. Speaking in broken English he then asked where my father worked but, when he asked for my address, I didn't understand what he meant. He repeated, "Where your house?" I was frightened and confused but answered by pointing in the direction of the hospital. He could see that I was frightened so, lowering the tone of his voice, he said, "Don't be a silly boy in the future," then ordered me to go home right away.

I crossed the road to see if Johnny Eastoe was still hiding in the ditch but he was nowhere to be seen. I guessed that he had made his getaway while I was being dealt with at the guardroom. Things were looking bad for me. I had been caught taking pot-shots with my catapult t at the Gurkha sentries and my details had been taken. Now my father would find out that I had disobeyed his orders not to play with Johnny Eastoe and, worse still, had left the house without permission and fired a catapult at the sentries.

Making my way home I pondered my fate. I began to feel that I could never face Johnny Eastoe again - not after letting him down so miserably - and so I resigned myself to facing whatever punishment was coming.

I waited in fear for the rest of the day, not saying a word to anyone. At times like this I would always seek Nana's company and this time she must have noticed me hanging around her. As the day went on and time for Father to come home drew nearer, she looked at me and said, "What have you been getting up to this time my son?" I said, "Nothing," at first but then realised that, if I were going to rely on her help later, I would have to tell her what happened. So I did. There was a short pause and then she said, "You have to stop these shenanigans, Ian. I won't be able to save your skin every time. Go and play and I'll see what I can do." Nothing was said when Father came home and I kept well out of the way. Nor was anything mentioned during dinner that night. The next day Nana said that the *Jemedar* (Guard Commander) had probably forgotten all about it and that I had got away with it this time, by the skin of my teeth!

Military Social Life

The grown-ups seemed to be enjoying a good social life. They spent most evenings on the veranda, entertaining friends and neighbours, it being cooler on the veranda than in the house. The main topics of conversation usually centred on their Indian co-workers and their somewhat comical misuse of the English language. Father's voice would become louder as the evening went on and, when he ran out of things to say about his Indian workmates, he would ridicule Premhassi, who was always on hand to pour drinks and to clear up after they had gone to bed.

During the day Mum busied herself making out menus for Bansi and shopping lists for Premhassi to take to the army supply store and the bazaar. Mum also had to deal with the various vendors who would call at the house daily, offering fruit, vegetables, cooking oil and ice, as well as laundry services. In the afternoons she would rest, or invite some friends along for a hand of whist or bridge, or even a game of badminton on the front lawn, followed by afternoon tea.

Apart from the regular vendors, there was always the casual but persistent hawker trying desperately to persuade Mum to buy bed linen, towels or other household items. A steady stream of *mochis* (cobblers), *darzis* (tailors) and knife sharpeners would often call to ask if we were in need of their services. In addition to these there was also the snake charmer, the man with the dancing bear and the man with monkeys that performed tricks to the sounds of a *dug-dug* (small hand drum).

Once in a while Mum would join with some of the other army wives and go over to the Italian prisoner of war camp, where they held a regular game of 'Housie-Housie' (Bingo). To keep me out of mischief she would take me along with her. The Italians loved children and perhaps I reminded them of their own children back in Italy, as they wasted no time in spoiling me rotten. They would call me over, give me sweets and biscuits - even give me a bingo ticket and help me to 'play' the game. The numbers were first called in Italian and then in English. After attending these events for a while, I began to learn how to count in Italian. It greatly amused them when I repeated the numbers and they would embrace me saying, "Bravo, bambino!"

Every evening, at eight o'clock, the family would sit down to dinner. Our hands would be inspected for cleanliness and only then would we be allowed to sit at the table. We were to remain silent, unless spoken to by the elders. Mum would plate up a meal for each one of us in turn, asking if it were enough. Father would follow that by saying, "You will have to eat everything you asked for and remain at the table until you've finished it." He would also insist that we sit up straight and keep our elbows by our sides. If we were seen to put our elbows on the table our arms would be lifted and our elbows banged sharply on the table. Any sign of misbehaviour on our part would be met with admonishment. The servants would be on edge all the time; the cleanliness of the crockery and cutlery and their hands and clothing would come under close scrutiny and they were not permitted to enter the house wearing shoes. After dinner the whole family would take a walk along the main road, with Premhassi leading the way with a torch, in order to clear the road of any deadly wildlife.

During the monsoon season the drainage ditches on either side of the road would fill up with rain water and all the creepy-crawlies would find refuge on higher ground, or on the verandas of the house. It was Premhassi's job to go out onto the veranda with a torch at night and get rid of them. I would join him and watch him as he fearlessly trod on tarantulas with his bare feet and dealt with small snakes, scorpions and centipedes in the same way. He was also a crack shot with a tea towel, his technique being to hold it by the diagonal corners, wind it around, and then snap it on my behind. He never missed!

One evening, while we were having dinner, Premhassi became a hero. My mother had a habit of slipping off her shoes and crossing her ankles under her chair, while at the dinner table. Premhassi suddenly became stony-faced and said to her, in a calm voice, "*Arp ki pow neihi haillo, Memsahib. (Don't move your feet, Memsahib.)*" I heard the familiar snap of his tea towel and out from under her chair tumbled a large tarantula with a couple of its legs missing. It was on its back and struggling to survive when he caught up with it on the other side of the dining table and dispatched it with his bare foot. He said later that it had been only inches away from Mum's bare feet.

I got on well with Premhassi. He had the thankless job of finding me, catching me and taking me back to the house whenever I had misbehaved and gone on the run. He was probably about fifteen or sixteen years old at the time. His duties were to run errands, help in the kitchen, wait at table and perform the duties of a general dogsbody. His reward for all this was two new sets of clothes every year and an occasional treat to the bioscope (cinema), which he loved. He always tried to make me laugh by telling me silly stories and singing the latest Indian pop songs, which he had probably heard on one of his trips to the cinema.

One Sunday morning Premhassi was escorting Theo and me back from Sunday school and he must have felt unwell. He sat down on a culvert at the side of the road, holding both of us in a tight grip around the waist, and his eyes became fixed in a faraway gaze. Some Italian POWs passing in a *tonga* noticed this and, realising that something was wrong, tried to prise us away from him but he was reluctant to let go. I cannot remember what the final outcome was but we were later told by Nana that he had suffered a fit of some sort. I always teased him after that, by looking at him with my cheeks sucked in and my eyes crossed. He said, "One day you will be doing that and the wind will blow on your face and your face will stay like that." I believed him and stopped doing it!

Servants

Premhassi lived with his parents, Bansi and Lavinia, in the servants' quarters, which were situated about a hundred or more yards away from the back of our house. Our servants, in common with many others, were not paid much but were expected to consider themselves fortunate to have secured a roof over their heads, two sets of new clothes each year and perhaps enough money to afford some rice and dal! However it was not unheard of for them to help themselves to tea, sugar, flour, rice and other foodstuff that may have taken their fancy. I don't blame them!

It bears repeating that the people who worked as servants for Europeans and Anglo-Indians were usually converts to Christianity. Missionaries found it very easy to convert those of the lowest social caste, by telling them that becoming Christian would immediately free them of their 'untouchable' status. These were the people who were trained up to become servants to the European community. No self-respecting Hindu or Muslim would consider becoming a servant in a Christian household.

Apart from the *ayah*, cook and houseboy, who were permanent employees, there were other casual employees from the lowest castes who were engaged on a daily or part-time basis. There was the *bhunghi*, who did all the sweeping around the house, the *methar*, who came twice a day to turn out the thunder-boxes and chamber-pots, and the *maali*, who cut the grass and tended the garden. A *bhisti* (water carrier) provided the family with hot water for bathing twice a week and also lit the fire in the salamander and kept it topped up with hot water. A salamander is a large, galvanised metal container, much like a metal water butt but with a flue running through the middle and a firebox underneath. This was the only way of heating large volumes of water for bathing and most families in India used them.

More family incidents from this era come to mind: like the time Barbara, then only about four years old, toddled onto an already-fragile cover of the cesspit at the back of the house. It broke in two and she slid into the septic tank. She had to be taken to the hospital across the road to have her stomach pumped out. Another time I was badly scalded when I managed to run straight into one of the next-door neighbours' servants, carrying a pan of boiling milk from the kitchen into the house. They had to strip off all my clothes and run me over to hospital, naked.

Then there was the time when we awoke one morning to find that a colourful snake had taken up residence in the empty fireplace. Nana said that it was a carpet snake. It was not unusual for obnoxious creatures to enter the house, as most households would leave doors and windows open during the day to allow any available breeze to circulate. Venomous wildlife made their homes in the monsoon ditches, among the fallen leaves and dry grass which gathered in the bottom of them, but in the rains they would seek drier places to bed down. We were constantly being warned not to play in the ditches and never to put our hands into dark places. It was always drummed into us to knock our shoes on the backs of their heels; tarantulas and scorpions love dark places to curl up in.

Swimming Lesson

Most young boys knew how to make a catapult and, with some practice, become quite expert shots. Both Theo and I carried ours wherever we went. There was so much wildlife to take pot-shots at that nothing was spared. In fact, anything that stayed still long enough would be regarded as essential target practice! The quarry ranged from huge vultures to small birds and squirrels but a lot of the fun with a 'catty' was derived from the competition between us. Whenever a group of we children gathered together a target would be chosen and we would while away many an hour just taking turns and indulging in a bit of one-upmanship, coupled of course with a lot of hot air and bragging. It was quite an art though, as no two 'catties' were alike. Accuracy came from knowing exactly what your own 'catty' was capable of and of course your sense of judgement - that was if you were blessed with any!

Some time had passed since I had seen anything of Johnny Eastoe but one day I caught sight of him playing marbles with some *chokaras* (Indian boys), near to the servants' quarters. Now firstly, I was not allowed to mix with the *chokaras* and secondly, nor was I allowed to associate with Johnny, but the prospect of some excitement got the better of me and I managed to sneak away from the house unnoticed. I went over to where the game of marbles was in progress. At first Johnny seemed not to notice me, so I just stood and watched the game.

I was about to turn and go home when an argument broke out between Johnny and one of the *chokaras*. They began to exchange insults and hurl filthy language at each other, some of which I had never heard before. Suddenly, Johnny went for his 'catty', loaded it and fired at the *chokara's* bare feet, catching him on the ankle. The *chokara* fell to the ground clutching his ankle and began screaming and we all scattered in every direction.

Thinking back, I do not know why I started to run, as I was only a passive onlooker and I had only managed to run a few yards when I tripped and fell. Johnny turned around, came back and helped me up urging me, "This way, this way!" We ran towards the back of the Gurkha Regiment's married quarters. It was not until we stopped running that Johnny noticed I had grazed my knee, which was bleeding.

As we approached a standpipe to wash the blood off my knee, a Gurkha woman, who was filling a bucket with water, asked Johnny where we were going. He replied, "I'm taking him home to get his knee dressed." He was lying. We were unable to go back home as, by now, there would have been a posse of *chokara* parents looking for us. I had unwittingly implicated myself in the incident and would be judged to be guilty by association. We carried on walking behind the Gurkha married quarters, as Johnny said this would avoid having to pass by the guardroom. It was a steaming hot day. Johnny said, "I know, we'll go for a swim in the lake and by the time we get back the whole shemozzle will have been forgotten." That sounded exciting to me; I had never swum in the lake before.

We seemed to have been walking for quite some time, stopping occasionally to take pot-shots with our 'catties' at anything that presented itself. Then, as the lake came into view at a distance, I could see what looked like someone washing clothes. As we got closer, the size of the lake began to worry me. I had never been so near to such a large expanse of water. I asked Johnny, "Is the water deep?" "Only in the middle - not on the edges," he said. We were now standing on the edge of the lake. Not too far away there were some Indian children splashing about in the water, while a woman (probably their mother) was washing clothes.

Johnny wasted no time. He stripped off and got straight in but I stood on the side and watched him for a while. He began to splash about and make silly noises. Then, in up to his waist, he turned around and said, "Come on, get in, don't be scared!" I made gestures pretending I wasn't scared but my heart was racing, partly with excitement, but mostly with fear. This was to be the first time that I would dip my body in water deeper than the twelve inches which I was used to in a tin bath. I slowly began to take off my shoes and clothes. I noticed that my hands were trembling so much that I had difficulty undoing my shirt buttons, but eventually I managed to strip completely.

I slowly made my way forward to the edge of the water but, with all the green slime under the surface, I had difficulty knowing where to place my feet safely. For a moment I almost drew back but then Johnny shouted, "Come on!" Cautiously I put one foot in, then the other, and moved forward until the water was up to my knees. I started to laugh nervously then found myself yelling out, just like Johnny did. It always helps in times of fear and uncertainty to make a noise, a technique I learnt from being locked up in the 'go-down'! Soon I began to gain a little courage and went in deeper, until I was in up to my waist, but I was still uncertain about what to do next.

I looked over to where the Indian woman and kids were. The kids seemed to be splashing about in a relaxed manner and enjoying themselves, as was Johnny. I, on the other hand, was finding it difficult to muster my courage - let alone be relaxed - but I did cautiously wade in until the water was up to my chest. I then began to feel unsteady and suffered a sudden loss of confidence, so decided to turn and go back. In doing so I lost my balance and, with nothing to grab on to, my brain went into panic mode. I started to thrash about with my arms in an attempt to regain balance. I lost my footing and my head went under the water, causing me to take in a lungful of lake. My legs were searching frantically for a foothold of some sort but my sense of direction had deserted me. I was beginning to lose strength when suddenly I felt my foot touching something, which must have been the lake bottom. My body stiffened, which must have corrected my balance, and my head emerged. Still in a state of uncontrollable panic I was coughing and trying to take a breath at the same time.

I felt a hand grab me by the arm; it was the Indian woman. She uttered some words in Hindi and dragged me to the side and sat me on the large rock, where she had been doing her washing; I was still coughing and spluttering. Johnny came out of the water saying, "What happened? What happened?" I couldn't answer as I was still trying to regain my breath and coughing up water. There was another couple of minutes of coughing and spluttering until I finally started to calm down. After waiting a while to dry off we got dressed and started back in the direction of home.

We had come a long way and this gave me time to reflect on my big day of unplanned adventure. It could have ended in tragedy but the possible consequences did not even enter my mind at the time. Johnny, who lived further on from me, said, "Cheerio," and carried on his way.

It was not until our bungalow came into sight that it began to dawn on me that I had been away from home for most of the day. I had no idea of what time it was but I had an inkling that it might be quite late. I approached the bungalow from the back, by the servants' quarters, where my adventurous day had first begun. There was nobody around. I stopped and leaned against the wall for a while, then started off towards the kitchen, in the forlorn hope that nobody would have noticed my absence. On the way, I had to pass the 'go-down'; I glanced at it and the thought of having to spend time in there crossed my mind.

The kitchens to these quarters were situated away from the bungalow, with a covered walkway connecting them. I popped my head into the kitchen doorway and was greeted with a very angry-looking Bansi. *"Baba, vay you are go, alla peoples lokka you."* I soon got the message!

I turned on my heels, and was about to take off, when I ran straight into Premhassi. He grabbed me by the arm and gave me one of his sympathetic looks. "*Mere saath chalo* (Come with me)," while shaking his head in a way peculiar to Indians, which indicates neither yes nor no, but which always conveyed Premhassi's empathy. He guided me through the dining room and onto the veranda. Nana, Papa and Mum were seated. They all turned to look at me. My father was standing on the steps leading up to the veranda holding a large *neem* swish in his hand. "What have you got to say for yourself?" he barked. I was dumb-struck, my eyes fixed on the *neem* switch in his hand. "Haven't you got anything to say?" I hadn't. I was in the grip of that all too familiar feeling of intense guilt and fear, knowing that if I were to open my mouth it would be the signal for the thrashing to begin.

At that moment Nana broke the silence. "Do you realise how much trouble you've caused today son? The whole neighbourhood has been looking for you, and you've been gone all day. Apologise to your father!" My eyes were now fixed on the veranda floor. I remained silent and could not bring myself to look my Father in the eye. He had piercing green eyes that could set a haystack on fire with just one glance! "That will not be enough," said Father. Making a swift movement forward he grabbed me by the arm, dragged me off the veranda and onto the lawn where he could get a better swing and began shouting at me.

"You've been missing all day! You've had everybody frantically searching for you; your mother's been sick with worry - and you've nothing to say?"

The first whack landed on my behind, I jerked forward and began to yell and run in a circle, with Father holding onto my left arm. I don't know how long it lasted, or how many times the switch landed on my legs, back and behind, but I can say that the stinging pain was all too familiar. Eventually he let go of my arm and I ran a couple of steps before falling in a heap with my face landing on a bare, dusty patch of the lawn. I must have looked a sight lying there sobbing with the dust sticking to my tear-soaked face.

Nana picked me up, took me to the bathroom, and cleaned me up. She smeared Germolene on the weals on my body and dressed me in some clean clothes. I was still lying on my bed, face down, sobbing and feeling sorry for myself, when a soft voice said, "*Chalo, khana khow.* (Come, eat your dinner.)" It was Premhassi but I pretended that I hadn't heard him. He placed a hand on my shoulder repeating, "Come, eat your dinner." He helped me up and took me to my chair in the dining room where the rest of the family were eating in silence. It would have been too painful for me to sit, so Premhassi removed the chair and I stood at the table.

He put a plate of food in front of me and I stood, hands by my side and head bowed over the plate, making no attempt to pick up the cutlery. My Father's irate voice boomed, "Straighten up." I straightened up with a jerk, instinctively. "Now eat your dinner and think yourself lucky not to have been sent to bed without any." At first I picked over my food, in a gesture of would-be defiance. However, I had not eaten or drunk anything all day (apart from a large gulp of stagnant lake-water) so the necessity for sustenance must have kicked in and I finished my dinner in record time.

The following day Nana called out to me; I found her sitting on her bed, brushing her long hair. She looked at me, told me to turn around, then lifted up my shirt, stroking the weals on my back saying, "You're such a silly boy. Now, you'd better tell me where you were and what you were doing yesterday, because when your father gets home in the evening he's going to want to know and I don't want you to have to go through that again." I began mumbling, searching for words that could have excused me for the previous day's antics. She stopped me saying, "You'd better tell me the truth, or I won't be able to help you out of this silly mess."

I began, "I was watching Johnny Eastoe playing marbles with some *chokaras* by the servants' quarters and he had a fight with one of them and got him in the foot with his 'catty'. They chased us and we went for a swim in a lake." A look of horror came over Nana's face.

"Oh good God!" she said, "You mean the lake by the Detachment Camp?" "I don't know," I said. "But that lake is out of bounds to all military personnel!" I didn't know what she meant. "I might have known that Johnny Eastoe was involved; you would never have gone anywhere on your own. That lake contains some of the most venomous water snakes - that's why it's out of bounds." I still didn't understand what 'out of bounds' meant so I just stayed silent.

That evening both Mum and Nana sat on the veranda waiting for my father to come home. I stayed well out of the way but within earshot. Nana and Papa's bedroom windows faced the veranda so, from their bedroom, I took up position, sitting on the edge of Nana's bed with the window ajar. After what seemed like ages, I heard my father greeting Mum and Nana. The usual preliminaries over, the conversation developed quickly into a discussion about my outrageous misbehaviour the previous day. Nana told Father that I had confessed to what had happened. Mum and Nana began to try to humour and reason with my father. My ears pricked up. I didn't understand some of the words they were using but I heard the phrase 'persistent disobedience' at least a couple of times.

The discussion soon turned into a lecture from my father to Mum and Nana, with a directive not to undermine his authority with regard to discipline within the family. "I know where the little bugger was yesterday," he said. "There was a notice on Part Two Orders at the hospital this morning, warning all personnel of the dangers of allowing family members to bathe in the lake. Some European children were spotted bathing there yesterday by the Guard Commander at the Detachment Camp Guardroom. He detailed a *sapahi* (Indian soldier) to investigate but the children had gone before the man arrived. That boy has been warned several times never to leave the house or go anywhere without permission. How many times has he been told not to mix with the Eastoe boy? If he continues to defy me I will have to send him somewhere where they will knock the devil out of him. The only answer is to get him into a tough boarding school."

What War?

It was May 1945, I was now seven years old and there was an air of excitement around. Nana said the war was over.

WAR! What war? I didn't know anything about a war. Things seemed to have become a little quieter and I noticed my father's absence, asking Nana, "Isn't Father coming home any more?" She told me, "Your Father has been sent to another place for a while and we will be moving to another house shortly." The quarters we were occupying were reserved for hospital staff only, so we had to move to quarters for families of fathers who were 'on detachment' (that is: temporarily posted elsewhere). The new quarters were situated in a more secure location, right in the middle of the Duke of Wellington Regiment's Barracks. These bungalows were brick-built and much more substantial in construction than the ones near the hospital. They each had a large veranda and proper electric ceiling fans in every room. A tarmac road separated them from the many lines of barracks, which were similar in construction to our quarters. On the end of our block was an 'MI Room' – the Medical Inspection, or First Aid room. Many of the army-approved trades such as tailors, cobblers, barbers and *chai wallahs* (tea vendors) occupied a row of buildings nearby. The Army even had its own dairy that delivered milk and butter on a daily basis, as there was no way of preserving it for any more than twenty-four hours.

This was a much more exciting and vibrant location. From the veranda we could watch the soldiers being drilled on parade and I would make frequent visits to the *darzi's* (tailor's) and the *mochi's* (cobbler's) shops. I became fascinated with the work they were doing and would sit quietly for long periods watching intently - even returning on a daily basis to follow the progress of a pair of shoes or the making of a shirt. I made mental notes on how the sole of a shoe was stitched to the upper, or how the collar and cuffs of a shirt were attached to the body. The craftsmen were very patient with me and were even willing to demonstrate how to make best use of certain tools. This interaction had the benefit of improving my Urdu/Hindi, as it was the only way to communicate. They spoke little or no English.

On trips to the bazaar I would look out for the artisans sitting in front of their shops, beating metal or carving wood. I was fascinated to see a tinsmith cutting up an empty kerosene can and turn it into a mug or some other utensil. If I spotted any workmen on the camp I would make a beeline for them and just stand and watch. There was also a carpenter's shop on the camp, which the 'Tommies' used during their leisure time. Sometimes, when I went along to watch them, they would make wooden toys and give them to me. I had no idea then that my thirst for practical knowledge (as opposed to academic learning) would become my sole means of self-expression and also the basis on which I would eventually earn my living. My keen observation of methods of manufacture, and my close scrutiny of practical processes, was to become a driving force in my life. To become even reasonably competent in any practical task seemed to fill me with excitement and confidence.

By contrast, making sense of the written word - reading and writing - seemed impossibly difficult and any effort on my part would always end in frustration. Yet I could see that other boys and even girls, much younger than me, seemed not to have these difficulties. I suspect it was a subconscious decision that caused me to reject that essential branch of the learning process, in favour of what I thought was a more satisfying way of expressing myself.

Unsurprisingly, I was the first child in our family to learn to ride a bicycle. While Father was away Mum got a part-time job in a government office as a stenographer and she hired a bicycle to get her to work and back. I would wait for her to come home and, when I thought she was busy in the house, I would steal the bike. After a series of disasters I eventually learnt to ride it. It was a ladies' bike so I was able to straddle the low crossbar and ride in a standing position, as I had seen older Indian kids do. The handlebars were too high for me to operate the brakes efficiently, resulting in quite a few mishaps. Hence I became a regular visitor to the camp 'MI'. There they would daub my grazed knees and elbows with strong iodine, which brought tears to my eyes. I would go away, resolving not to let it happen again. Naturally, before long, I would be back in there again, having my wounds tended to.

I also put my mind to learn how to maintain the bicycle and would use Papa's '3-in-1' gun oil on the wheel hubs and other working parts. I could also replace the chain whenever it came off. When Mum first discovered that I was riding her bike without her knowledge she was angry but, being a 'softie', she soon relented and would let me ride it up and down the main road between the barracks and the quarters, where she could keep an eye on me. Of course, if I thought she was too busy to notice, I would sneak off and go much further away…

It became a huge confidence boost for me that, aged just seven, I could ride a grown-up's bicycle. I enjoyed it when people saw me riding up and down the road and made comments about such a young boy riding a full-sized bicycle; it would make me feel great. One day, while riding along the road, a couple of off-duty 'Tommies' from the barracks called out to me to go over to them. I went over and they said, "Who taught you to ride that bike?" "I taught myself!" I said. They seemed amused, looked at each other and smiled. One of them went into the barrack-room and came out with a handful of sweets, handed them to me then patted me on the head saying, "Well done, Sonny Boy!" I remember experiencing a gush of pride and an urgent need to show off. I pedalled away at speed, with a grin on my face like a new moon.

Later that day, while out looking for something to fire my 'catty' at, I put a hand in my pocket to take out a sweet and was met with a vicious attack from the largest hornet I have ever seen. The hornet had attached itself to the outside of my pocket and, having been attracted by the scent of the sweets, had somehow managed to sting me on the second finger of my right hand. The pain was excruciating! As I looked at my finger a drop of blood dripped from it and I panicked, running home in tears.

By the time I got home my hand had begun to swell up and my finger had turned a nasty shade of grey/blue. The first person I saw was Papa, so I ran towards him with my arm outstretched shouting, "Hornet! Hornet!" Papa took a look at it and asked, "Are you sure it was a hornet?" I nodded, trying to choke back the tears. There was a puzzled look on his face. "I think we'd better let the nurse take a look at this," he said. He took me to the MI Room. The male nurse on duty and I were well acquainted. Papa held my hand out while the nurse inspected it. "Oh my gosh! Are you certain it was a hornet?" he asked. I nodded several times and then said, "I saw it." "Ok!" he said, "But I would like the opinion of a doctor. Wait here."

By now my hand had begun to look like an inflated rubber glove and the swelling had advanced up to my wrist. I kept wincing with pain trying to stifle the sobs. While we were waiting for the doctor to arrive Papa kept looking at my hand with that same puzzled look on his face, shaking his head slightly. My sounds of distress had attracted the attention of a female nurse, who came over and did her best to comfort me but I was only half listening to her. The doctor eventually arrived to inspect my hand; his reaction was the same as the nurse's. Placing his crooked index finger under my chin, he tilted my head up so that he could look me in the eye and repeated the very same words that Papa and the nurse had said. I nodded several times in irritation at his doubting tone. "Why don't they believe me?" I asked myself.

"All right, all right," said the doctor, then turned to the male nurse and mumbled something to him while they were walking away. The nurse soon returned with a kidney tray in one hand and the now-familiar brown bottle of iodine in the other. After persuading me to cooperate with him, he cleaned the wounded area with 'ether-meth' and applied the strong iodine to my finger and then to the rest of my arm, right up to the elbow. While he was doing this both he and Papa were agreed that it looked a bit too severe to be just a hornet sting and he told Papa that it might be a good idea to apply ice to the hand and arm to reduce the swelling. He added that he should bring me back later that evening for a check-up. I spent the rest of the afternoon sitting on the veranda with my hand wrapped in some muslin with crushed ice in it and feeling very sorry for myself!

Nevertheless, the words of the 'Tommies' kept ringing in my ears. "Well done, Sonny Boy." They must have awakened some deep psychological reaction within me. I was hardly mature enough to rationalise it at the time but, looking back, I now realise that those simple words were a powerful endorsement and that hearing them had boosted my self-confidence enormously. Unfortunately, this brought with it an increase in my challenging behaviour. With my father out of the away I started to become very cheeky to Mum, Nana and even to Papa; a number of defiant episodes followed. Papa hardly ever said a harsh word to me but even he began to register his disapproval. My mother, being so soft, wasn't able to cope with my behaviour. Nor was Nana, so they had to resort to threatening me with the same old phrase, "You wait till your father comes home."

Barnes High School

Mum called out to Theo and me one day; she was standing on the veranda and behind her stood a man, with what looked like a sewing machine on his shoulder. "The *darzi* (tailor) is going to measure you up for new clothes," Mum said. "Is it going to be Christmas soon?" I asked; we usually only got new clothes at Christmas. "No," she said. "You're going to need them because you'll be going to a boarding school soon." I don't recall any adverse reaction to this news on my part. I think I was more excited at the prospect of being able to watch the *darzi* at work on our veranda.

A couple of days later the *mochi* (cobbler) arrived. He made us stand on a clean sheet of paper and, with a pencil, drew the outline of our feet, to give him some idea of what size last he would need to use. He handed a book containing shoe patterns to Mum. She selected one and pointed to it; he nodded his head saying, *"Kia rung memsahib?* (What colour madam?)" She answered, *"Kala* (Black*)." "Gee hann memsahib.* (Yes madam.)"

For the next few days I was in heaven, spending every minute I could, flitting from the *darzi* to the *mochi,* watching intently as they both sat cross-legged on the veranda floor, with their work in front of them. They seemed to enjoy their work so much, occasionally stopping to have short conversations and even singing under their breath while working. I would bring them cups of water or tea when they asked and took messages from them to Mum, as my Urdu was better than hers - she seemed to struggle with it at times. Once the clothes and shoes were complete, we tried them on for fit and then they were packed away.

In the midst of all these preparations my father arrived home without warning. Unsure whether Mum would carry out all of the threats she had issued during his absence, I stayed well out of the way and waited to see how things developed. After a couple of days of excitement and merry-making by the grown-ups, it seemed that nothing drastic was going to happen to me, so I began to relax a little but always stayed alert for the mere mention of my name.

With our trunks packed, and dressed in our new clothes, we were off to boarding school for a second time. Nana said that this one was situated just outside a place called Deolali, (yes, it does exist!), where my father had been posted. She added that Father may be able to come up and see us sometimes. For my part, only the prospect of another rail journey excited me. The thought of being separated from the family didn't seem to bother me – although I certainly had no yearning for an education. At least I wouldn't have my father breathing down my neck while I was at school. I could probably tolerate him visiting us, as long as he brought some tuck with him. Theo on the other hand, was probably more affected by the separation. He got on much better with Father than I did, as he was far less of a challenge to his authority.

The approach to Barnes High School was through a gated entrance, with a bit of an uphill climb, and the *tonga* driver had to urge the poor horse on with an occasional lash of the whip. A building which we passed on the right turned out to be the infirmary and opposite that was the Headmaster's house. In front and to the right were some large three-story buildings, where Theo and I would be spending the next few months. In a play area to the right and behind the building I spotted what looked like a game of hockey in progress. I kept my eyes on the game and became oblivious to everything else.

Soon, an older girl who introduced herself as Cynthia Ashkins led myself, Theo, Mum and Father up some stairs and gave us a short tour of what was to be mine and Theo's living quarters. There were about eight beds on either side of the long room. At the far end was a selected space which Cynthia said was hers, adding that she was the Dormitory Prefect and that she would be looking after our needs out of classroom hours. Conditions here were a huge improvement on our first boarding school. The bathroom floor and walls were covered with white glazed tiles and there was even indoor plumbing with washbowls and proper flush toilets - but no baths tubs. We were to wash ourselves down by filling the washbowls and the water ran off into a central, covered drain.

Cynthia said that she would arrange to have our luggage brought up to the dormitory. As the *tonga* was waiting to take Mum and Father back to the train station, she told us that we should now go and say goodbye. When we got downstairs, my attention was again drawn to the hockey game, which was still going on. Then I heard my name being called. I turned to see my mother embracing Theo - they were both crying. Father said in his usual stern voice, "We have to go now," adding, "Just behave yourselves and keep your noses clean. You'll soon settle in. We'll write to you and I may be able to visit you from time to time." Mum then reached out to hug me as well. Without saying anything, she drew me towards her and kissed my cheek. Her tears moistened my face and I began to feel emotional but managed to hold back, only just squeezing out a smile. I wiped Mum's tears from my face with the back of my hand.

We stood and watched the *tonga* go out of sight, then turned and looked at each other not knowing what to do next. For a moment I thought of putting my arm around Theo's shoulder to comfort him, but quickly realised that it might start me off crying and the kids playing hockey would see me and brand me a bit of a sap. A show of emotion would be looked on as a sign of weakness. Although my insides felt like jelly I realised that I was going to have to adopt some kind of hard front.

We stood and watched the kids playing hockey for a while - Theo still choking back the sobs. One of the kids then ran towards me and asked if I'd like to borrow his hockey stick. I grabbed it with glee, leaving him talking to Theo. I had no idea of the rules of the game, so I just waded in trying to get a swipe at the ball whenever it came within striking distance. After a short while, I noticed that there was one character, a ginger-haired boy, who seemed to be doing a lot of shouting and telling the rest of them what to do. I can't remember how or when the game finished but it must have helped me to cope with my emotions and to break the ice with my peers.

Although my brother and I were latecomers to the term, we seemed to settle into our dormitory routine without much fuss. Looking out from my window in the front of the building to the distance, I could see a road that was probably the road we had travelled along on our way to the school. At the back of the building there was the flat area, where I had played hockey earlier. This extended with a gentle slope down towards what looked like a narrow, slow-running river. It had been dammed with thick walls in two places, about fifty yards apart. This created a section of calm water. I later discovered that it was used as the school swimming pool and was referred to as 'The Duck Pond'. Still looking out of the back of the building to our left was the senior boys' school and dining hall. To the right, and upstairs, in the same building as ours, was the senior girls' school. Our block was central, with the dormitories on the upper floors and classrooms on the lower floor.

I think I must have felt quite at ease here. I can't remember anyone making a fuss when I occasionally wet my bed and the discipline seemed to be quite relaxed; I also can't recall any of the staff being unduly severe - although later, I did get six strokes of the cane on my behind from the Headmaster for throwing stones into a tree! Unfortunately one of the stones landed right in front of him while he was cycling along the path that ran along the other side of the tree; I hadn't noticed him!

Bullyboy

The classroom had never been my favourite place; I always felt ill at ease during lessons. Reading and writing were still a struggle for me and I wasn't able to keep up with the other kids. At first the teachers tried to be helpful, saying that if I didn't understand anything, I was merely to ask. However, I was reluctant to approach them, firstly, because I wasn't able to explain what the problem was and secondly, although I felt obliged to nod my head in agreement, I didn't understand the explanations! The other kids seemed to have no trouble copying what was written on the blackboard and would laugh at my inability to comprehend. Eventually the teachers must have lost interest as they showed little concern for my lack of progress.

The garrison where my father was based must have been fairly nearby. At times, personnel used the school's dining hall with its large stage for ENSA shows (ENSA or Entertainments National Service Association, being the organisation for entertaining the armed forces). On these occasions pupils would be permitted to watch the first half of the show from a balcony at the back of the hall, before being marched off to bed.

My father was able to visit us on the occasional weekend, bringing with him what he called 'egg banjos' (fried egg sandwiches). I have to say that I looked forward to these visits, mostly because I was permanently hungry and eager to sink my teeth into some extra food. Being pleased to see my father was not something I was used to but those few occasions were the exception.

On one of his visits I plucked up the courage to confide in him about a recurring problem that I could not seem to resolve; it was the ginger-haired boy who had been shouting all the orders at the hockey game on the day we arrived. His name was George Whittle and he had an older brother in the senior school. This he imagined gave him dominion over the rest of us. He would claim and keep other pupils' property if he fancied it. If anyone mustered the nerve to object they would be met with violence, or even torture - arm twisting, punches to the stomach and upper arms or ear tweaking, all enthusiastically cheered on by his gang of followers, of course.

Like most of the other kids, I had learnt to keep out of George Whittle's way, but there was always the anticipation of his unwanted attention whenever he was close by. He seemed to generate a feeling of fear in me, similar to that which I experienced with my father. I became obsessed with his antics and felt sympathy for the victims of his reign of terror. Although I was unable to explain my feelings to my father at the time, I think he understood and sensed that the situation was troubling me. He began to counsel me that boarding schools could be rough places for young boys and that they had to learn to look after themselves. He said that parents could not intervene in such matters, adding that each boy must find his own way to deal with such problems.

He then went on to relate some of the tough situations that he had had to face during his boarding school days, hoping, I think, to instil some courage in me. But then came the bombshell! "Why don't you pick a fight with this bully?" he said. "Even at the expense of getting a hiding, he can't hurt you that much. Do it when there's a teacher or a grown-up nearby, so that they can intervene if things get out of control. It would at least show him and his mates that you're not afraid of him." I listened but said nothing back. I felt slightly unburdened but I had very mixed feelings about picking a fight with George Whittle and his cronies.

George Whittle had never picked on me, or perhaps I had escaped his attention because I disliked him and avoided his company. With my father's words fresh in my ears I began to look out for opportunities to put this advice into action. However, each time a possibility presented itself my heart would pound against my rib cage; my courage would desert me, and I would feel weak and nauseous. I would walk away, chiding myself and resolving that next time I would summon up the courage to act.

A craze for making peashooters from the branches of the papaya tree had developed among some of the older boys and one such tree grew at the back of our dormitory block. Spotting that, with some difficulty, daring and dexterity the branches could be reached from the upstairs bathroom window, I managed to break off a branch from the tree and fashioned two good peashooters from it. I kept what I considered to be the best one and gave the other to Wilbur Page, whose penknife I had borrowed to make them.

Wilbur and I were now the only juniors to have peashooters, a state of affairs that inevitably did not go unnoticed by George Whittle. Putting into action his well-practised methods of extortion he 'became the owner' of (i.e. stole from Wilbur) the only peashooter in the junior school, apart from mine. The following day George, armed with his new acquisition, began to have some fun in class. He chewed pieces of blotting paper, made pellets from them and began shooting them around the classroom at random. The teacher spotted him and confiscated the peashooter. Within a short space of time George was standing by me asking, "Where's your peashooter, then?" I replied that I had left it in the dorm, at which he just walked away, murmuring something. That was the first time he had ever spoken to me directly. I said nothing but felt intimidated and sensed that there was trouble ahead.

Shortly after this encounter, it was playtime. The playground was in front of the school block, surrounded by ornamental trees. At one end, there was a large brass bell, suspended from two metal posts with a bar across the top. A short length of rope hung from the striker. At the end of playtime a teacher would sound the bell or ask the nearest pupil to do so. On this occasion I happened to be the nearest one to the bell, so the teacher asked me to ring it. I ran forward, grabbed the rope and tugged enthusiastically. Just as I stopped, I felt the force of a kick in my backside, accompanied by the unmistakable sound of George Whittle's voice saying, "Oi! Who said that you could ring the bell?"

Like a flash, I swung round. Anger exploded inside me and, without a second thought, I unleashed a 'straight right' to his head, catching him full force on the left side of his mouth and knocking him to the ground. His cronies scattered in every direction. Giving him no time to recover, I jumped on him and, straddling his chest, continued to rain rapid blows to his face, until blood smeared his mouth and nose. With me sat on his chest he was unable to move much but he tried in vain to fend me off, shouting, "Stop! Stop! I give up! I give up!" His pleas for mercy bounced off the red mist of pent-up anger in me. I was not in a benevolent mood and I had only just started. I was beginning to enjoy my moment of triumph when I felt a hand tugging at my shirt collar and a voice shouting, "Stop it! Stop it!" It was the teacher. She pulled me off George, ordered me to stand by the bell, then picked him up and placed a handkerchief over his mouth and nose. He was crying like a baby!

While I was standing by the bell, watching the teacher attending to George, a feeling of intense relief came over me and an uncontrollable grin spread over my face. The faces in the small crowd of pupils that had gathered also had a look of barely restrained glee. Back in the classroom I was ordered to stand by the blackboard, while George's face was being cleaned up. When the teacher returned with him she grabbed us both by the arm demanding, "Now what was that all about?" George just about managed to mutter, through a pair of swollen and split lips, that I had attacked him for no reason but the teacher cut him short. She said that she had seen the incident and that he was as much to blame as I was. She then made us apologise to each other and sent us to our desks.

When I got back to my dormitory that day Cynthia Ashkins summoned me to her space at the end and questioned me about the incident. As I started to relate the story I noticed the beginning of a smile appearing on her face; I think she may have felt relieved that a festering problem in her dormitory had been resolved.

After the fight in the playground with George Whittle I enjoyed a period of minor popularity amongst my peers and, looking back on it, my self-confidence seemed to improve. My father's formula for dealing with such matters may have begun to make its impression. From then onwards, whenever I was faced with any such situation, I felt better able to deal with my fears. I can't say that I was conscious of any big change but my willingness to challenge certainly grew a little stronger.

I can't remember learning anything relating to the 'three Rs' during my brief stay at this school, though I think the George Whittle incident may have taught me a valuable lesson in human relations, i.e. 'the power of fear and the fear of power'. I believe that this particular incident was the origin of my underlying resentment towards anyone invested with power and authority, perceived or otherwise.

All Change

No sooner had we settled in at Barnes than we were told that we would be going to a different school. My father arrived one day to tell us that he had put our names down for the new school some time ago and that we needed to get there right away, in order to secure a place for the next year. The school was called The Lawrence Royal Military School, Sanawar. The exciting thing about this particular journey would be riding on the miniature railway for part of the way. Everything seemed to happen so rapidly that I can hardly remember anything, apart from the ride on the miniature railway of course!

On arrival at the school, I was placed in PD (Preparatory Department), which was situated some distance away from the main boys' school, where Theo had been placed. This was probably because, being under eight, I was too young for the main school.

I settled quite well into a dormitory with other boys, who were all about my own age. However, the classrooms were mixed - boys and girls - hence a lot of teasing went on! As an example, one day I was dared by some of the other boys during class to kiss one of the girls. Always eager to accept a challenge, I selected one of the quieter girls, plonked myself beside her and planted a kiss on her cheek. Not realising that the teacher had seen my prank, I quickly returned to my desk with a big grin on my face. Before I could get there, my teacher grabbed me by the arm and marched me out of the classroom, down a corridor and into a room where there was a stern-looking woman sitting behind a desk. The two women had a hasty discussion and, after a while, they both looked at me. Then one of them said, "Go back to the classroom." A short time later I was told that I would be joining my brother - at the boys' school!

The next morning, one of the Indian ladies took me down to the infirmary with my belongings and handed me over to a much older boy, dressed in khaki army uniform. He looked like an officer, wearing one of those brown leather belts that have a strap running from it and over the shoulder, along with a Gurkha type bush hat. Some paperwork was given to him and he told me to stand by the wall with my belongings, saying that he would come and fetch me later. I could see some other younger boys in army uniform beginning to form two lines.

The older boy, who spoke in loud tones to the younger ones, looked in my direction and said, "Come here you, and fall in with the rest of them." Soon we were marching along a dry mud road, which seemed to go on forever. My suitcase began to get heavier by the minute and my knee kept knocking against it, preventing me from keeping up with the other boys. Consequently I began to fall behind. Suddenly a loud voice said, "Come on you, you're going to have to buck up your ideas." It was the older boy, who was glaring at me in a menacing way.

When we finally got to the boys' school I was led across a cobbled open space and along a walkway into a long dormitory. There were iron beds along both sides and wooden chests placed at the foot of each bed. On top of the chests were blankets and sheets folded neatly in a rectangular shape, alternate sheets and blankets stacked like a slice of chocolate cake, with layers of cream, then wrapped neatly around in a blue patterned counterpane on the outside. At either end of the long room were doors; I followed the boy down the dormitory to a door at the opposite end from where we had entered. He knocked and we waited until a heavily-built woman, who spoke with a strange accent greeted us. A short conversation took place between her and the older boy; then I was told to stand by one of the empty beds and they both disappeared. A short while later they reappeared with blankets, bed linen, pyjamas and some clean clothes. The woman told me to get changed and that she would be back to see me later. The older boy left and I did not see him again after this.

I got changed and began to take in my surroundings. The inside of the dormitory looked just like the ones at the barracks, on the camp back in Meerut, while on the outside it was a two-story building with balconies running the full length of the upper storey on both sides. At the back of the building, a stairway led from top to bottom. The whole school was built on a steep hillside and the balcony overlooked a deep valley. On the lower floor there was another dormitory. A narrow strip of land, covered in fine gravel, ran along the length of the building and about twenty yards beyond that there was a long corrugated tin roofed shed-like building. Later, I was to discover that this was the washhouse and toilets. Much further down the hill was a large space which looked like a sports field built into the hillside and surrounded by a high mesh fence.

My survey of this scene was interrupted when a shrill voice summoned me back into the dormitory. It was the woman with the strange accent. "Come here; let me have a look at you. My word, you look like a sack of potatoes my boy. NOW!" she shouted, leaning forward and in a voice that rocked me back on my heels. "You call me Mrs Woon! You 'ear? You are now in the boys' school and in Outram House. I'm your House Mistress; I'll expect you to keep yourself clean and tidy at all times and I don't stand for any bad behaviour or bad manners. Do you understand?' "Yes, Miss," I replied. "It's Mrs Woon!" she yelled back. "Don't you forget it!" The volume and tone of her voice, with its strange accent, left me in no doubt that she must never be disobeyed.

"You can stay here for now but, when all the boys come down for lunch, you go along with them and they'll show you where to go. After lunch, report to your prefect. His room's there." She pointed to the other end of the dormitory then disappeared back in her room, slamming the heavy wooden door behind her. I was left in a state of confusion and apprehension. I tried sitting on the edge of the bed for a while but couldn't settle. I began to tiptoe down the centre of the dormitory, trying not to make too much noise on the rough wooden floor, until I got to the opposite end of the building, my head twitching from side to side trying to take everything in.

I took up a position in a doorway facing uphill. I could see the walkway leading from the dorm that led up some steps to another building - the ones that I had been led down earlier. A spark of courage led me to take a few steps onto the balcony, where I leaned against the banister to survey my surroundings. After what seemed like ages I saw some boys, passing in dribs and drabs, on the other side of the walkway; soon the place was swarming with boys of different ages and sizes.

What looked like a man in officer's uniform came down the walkway. I froze. As he approached me he said, "Are you the boy Smith?" I nodded, not knowing how to address him. "Are you?" "Yes sir," I said. "That's better. Speak up when you're spoken to." "Sorry sir," I said. Pointing up and to the right, he told me, "Go and stand over there by the water tank and see if you can find your brother when he comes for lunch. He'll show you where to go. Then after lunch, see me in there." He pointed in the direction of his room. He had obviously been forewarned of my arrival.

I made my way along the walkway and up some steps, which led on to a building with a veranda. To the right, there was an open cobblestone terrace, surrounded by a stone wall, where everyone seemed to be heading. I stood to one side next to an open water tank, hoping to get a glimpse of Theo among the passing lines of boys. Soon the procession became a trickle but I still hadn't spotted Theo. A man appeared, dressed in civilian clothes, with a black cloak draped over his shoulders. He approached me saying, "Why are you standing here boy?" "I'm looking for my brother sir," I replied. "Well you're not going to find him by just standing here are you?" I started to explain but he cut me short. "Come with me." I followed him through a crowd of boys standing in lines, facing yet another building. He stopped when we got to the very last line, which consisted of the smallest kids. "I think you are more likely to find him here," he said, gesturing towards them. I was still looking down the line when a voice from behind me said, "Get on the end of the line and go into the dining hall when they go in." It was the big boy dressed like an officer, who had found me on the walkway. I was soon to learn that he was a prefect.

It wasn't until I got into the dining hall and sat down with the other boys - on the end of a long bench, at an equally long table - that I spotted Theo. He was halfway down on the opposite side; he acknowledged me with a nod of his head as I waved. The big boy sat at the top of the table, dishing out the food onto plates and passing them down the table. Most of the boys were too busy eating to take any notice of me.

After lunch, Theo and I met up outside the dining hall and walked back together to the dormitory. We didn't have much to say to each other, but then we never did anyway. I told him that I had to see the prefect. "You mean Ralph Jones?" said Theo. "I don't know his name," I replied. "Well, that's his room there and he's the prefect." I duly took up my position outside his door and, when he finally arrived, Ralph called me into the room.

He began by introducing himself as the prefect of Outram House, adding that I would be answerable to him at all times. He followed that with a long list of do's and don'ts, his voice sounding a little less harsh now. He concluded by telling me that I must learn to keep myself clean and tidy at all times and to become independent, saying, "As long as you behave yourself, we will get along fine."

He then led me out into the dormitory and summoned a boy by the name of Victor Isaacs. He told Victor to keep an eye on me and to show me what to do, adding, "But don't mother him." There were so many instructions and rules to remember; the end of the day couldn't come too soon for me. However, before I could sleep, I had to polish my shoes and make my own bed. It was only then I discovered that the mattress and pillow I was to sleep on were stuffed with pine needles…

Crime and Punishment

I awoke the next morning to the all-too-familiar feeling of soggy pyjamas and bedclothes but this time they didn't seem to be all that soggy. While I had been at the preparatory school the staff had dealt with the situation but here I didn't know what to do. I followed the other boys to the ablution block downstairs. When I got back Victor told me that I would have to strip my bed, fold the mattress back in half and make a bed box, saying that he would show me this time but I would have to do it myself in future. I stripped the sheets off the bed and folded the mattress back in half. It was then that Victor spotted the wet patch under the bed. The pee had gone straight through the pine needles in the mattress and on to the floor. No wonder the bed hadn't felt too soggy!

He looked at me. "It looks like you've pissed the bed. Have you?" I nodded in silence. "I think you'd better tell the prefect," he said. Outside Ralph Jones' half-open door, I hesitated and then plucked up the courage to knock. "Yes?" he said. In an uncertain voice I replied, "I've wet my bed, Ralph." There was a slight pause. "Well what the hell do you want me to do about it? I can't help you; go and tell Mrs Woon." I scampered down to the other side of the dormitory, knocked on Mrs Woon's door and waited. Seconds later, the door opened and her face appeared.

Mrs Woon's looks were not her best asset. Her bloated red cheeks, large bulging eyes and snub nose were only made worse by a large toothless mouth and a bosom the size of a couple of watermelons. "Watchyouwant?" she blurted out. I repeated what I had told Ralph. Her eyelids dropped; she drew in a large breath and raised her head upwards. There was a pause. I waited for the eruption but it never came. She lowered her head slowly and said, "Right then, bring your wet things and leave them here," pointing to her doorstep. "I'll have your mattress changed later." You could have knocked me down with a feather!

The military regime took some getting used to. From early morning to lights out you were kept on your toes. Bugle calls had to be obeyed at the double and no excuses were accepted. After breakfast each morning, the entire boys' school would assemble on the parade ground. Prefects of each house would carry out inspections before we marched off to church. Uniform ranged from battle dress in winter months to khaki drill for summer. Headgear was either a cap or a Gurkha type hat. A belt of brown leather, with a brass buckle, was also worn. The cross-body belt or 'Sam Brown', which signified authority, was only worn by appointed prefects and gave them the appearance of officers.

Prefects took full advantage of the authority vested in them by issuing punishments of their own choosing. The most frequently used sanction for minor misdemeanours was to catch the offender a downward blow on the side of his head, just above the ear. This was delivered with a clenched fist, using the middle set of knuckles. The hollow sound it produced made the onlooker feel sick and the pain brought tears to the eyes of the recipient. The clenched fist was occasionally used in other ways - though well disguised and out of sight of others. Any noise made after lights out at night was met with silent punishments.

I came in for my fair share of these. It was now common knowledge that I sometimes wet the bed and, in an attempt to avoid doing it, I would try to stay awake for as long as possible after lights out. I noticed that Ralph Jones always stayed up later than the rest of us, in order to continue his studies and he would leave his door ajar. This would give me the opportunity to make use of the light coming from his room to see my way to the toilet. However, there were times when either I mistimed it or Ralph decided to have an early night. Bedtime was always a stressful time for me. The worry that I might wet the bed, coupled with the intense fear of the dark, would keep me awake long after every one had gone to sleep. Although Mrs Woon was forgiving at first, after a while she became less tolerant of my wet bed mishaps. I had to get up during the night to relieve myself, sometimes more than once.

There was a small, door-less and dimly lit room on the landing outside the dormitory, with a large metal bin placed in the centre. This was used as a night toilet. Always terrified of the dark, I would wait until one of the other boys was making their way to the toilet and join them. Some of them had the same fear and would do likewise, which resulted in occasional misjudgements and collisions - with each other or some inanimate object. One night, Ralph Jones was studying late when I needed the toilet so, as usual, I thought I would take advantage of the light coming through his partly-open door. Making my way towards the balcony, I misjudged the location of an empty bed just before the door and stumbled into it. I yelped, thus breaking one of Ralph Jones's cardinal rules, 'No noise after Lights Out', but I carried on to the toilet hoping he hadn't heard me.

On the way back I found him standing in his doorway. In a controlled way, he asked if it was me who had made a noise; I owned up. "Come here," he said in a quiet voice. He pointed to a spot outside his room near where his boots were, indicating that he wanted me to stand there. "Pick up my boots, one in each hand, and hold them up, arms stretched out in crucifix fashion, and keep them there until I tell you to stop." He left me and returned to his studies. Within a couple of minutes my arms began to lose strength and sag. With the strength gone from my arms I had to let go of the boots and they dropped to the floor, one after the other, with a loud thud.

Ralph came out of his room saying, "If you're too weak to hold them up, then you can polish them for the rest of the week. You're on fagging." I didn't know what he meant by 'fagging' and so, the next day, I asked Victor. He explained, "You'll have to report to Ralph every morning and he'll give you something to do in your spare time, like picking up litter in the school grounds, cleaning his boots or, on Saturdays and Wednesdays, you might have to fag down at the sports fields."

I had been having a bad spell of bed-wetting. One morning I was getting out of bed, when Ralph Jones walked down the middle of the dormitory, making sure that we were all up. He stopped, looked under my bed and saw a wet patch. "I'm getting fed up with this, you're supposed to be a big boy now but this is what little babies do. I'm going to give you something to remember that with," he announced.

He then told me to go and get a handful of some of the gravel from the yard downstairs and told the rest of the boys to go and get washed. When I returned he pushed my bed to one side with his foot, exposing the wet patch, and then ordered me to place the gravel on the wet patch. "Put the backs of your hands on the gravel, and kneel on the palms of your hands. Then keep repeating these words, 'I won't piss the bed, I shan't piss the bed, I won't piss the bed any more'."

I think I may have got half-way through the third repetition, when I couldn't stand it any more. Choking back the tears, I rolled over to one side, with much of the gravel still sticking to the backs of my hands. It was several days before the swelling and pins and needles in my hands subsided and I was able to grip my knife and fork properly.

Snakes and Fagging

As I said before, the school at Sanawar was built into the side of a hill. There were two sports grounds called Big Plain and Little Plain, which were built into the lower slopes of the school and were accessed by a steep winding footpath. The surface of Big Plain was compacted earth, covered with fine gravel, and was mostly used for cricket and hockey. Little Plain's surface was rough grass and was used for football. They both had very high, heavy chicken-wire fences on the down-slope sides.

Boys detailed to 'fag' during games periods, would be placed at strategic locations down the hillside to retrieve any stray balls that may go over the fence. A football posed little problem to track and find - however, a cricket ball was a different matter. If a ball went over the fence in your direction while you were on fagging and a prefect called your name, failure to find and retrieve it would result in you being placed on fagging for the next sports' session as well. I believe that one of these sessions was the origin of my phobia of reptiles.

After a couple of stints of fagging I had worked out a method of avoiding the more arduous search and recovery missions. I would take up a position next to a suitable bush and, when I heard the loud cheer from the spectators indicating that a ball was on its way over the high fence, I would quickly duck behind the bush to avoid being seen by the prefect. If the prefect later decided to question me, I could make the excuse that I was relieving myself.

On one of these occasions, during a cricket match, the usual loud cheers from the crowd erupted. I made a dash for the back of the bush I was standing near and then heard the name Gow being called. Ian Gow was the nearest boy to me, standing about twenty-five yards to my right. I saw him mouth an obscenity, then take off down the hillside. I watched him for a while as he struggled to keep his eyes on the cricket ball, while negotiating the steep valley below. When he was out of sight I allowed myself a moment of congratulation, then turned towards the hedge and almost buried myself in it in order to avoid being seen by any of the prefects.

However, something suddenly erupted like a coiled spring and out of the hedge came the head of a large black snake, with green under its gills, its tongue waving from side to side almost level with my eyes. It caused me to jerk backwards, lose my balance and fall to the ground, striking my left elbow on a rock. I'm not sure if it was the pain from my elbow, or the fright from the snake, but I had some kind of vocal, emotional outburst. (One of the other boys said later that I had been making noises like a constipated donkey!) My immediate reaction was to run up to the sports ground. It all happened so quickly that I can hardly remember doing so and I only stopped when I heard a voice saying, "Where the hell do you think you're going?" I didn't recognise the prefect but managed to squeeze out the words, "I'm feeling very sick." The look on my face must have convinced him of my distress. He made me sit on the stone wall surrounding the ground, saying that he would get someone to take me to the infirmary at the end of the game. The words were hardly out of his mouth, when the contents of my stomach splattered on the ground between my legs. I was kept in the infirmary overnight under observation and sent back to school in the morning. Ever since then, just the sight of any reptile reminds me of the intense terror I felt that day.

Mid-term Break

In addition to the daytime uniform, leisurewear was also provided at Sanawar. This consisted of light grey shorts and shirt, long grey socks and a pair of lightweight, leather thin-soled shoes. This attire was to be worn out of classroom hours for sport and during relaxation times. There was also a period of two weeks' holiday halfway through the term, when the whole school stood down. Some of the boys who lived not too far away from the school could go home to their families but the majority would have to spend this period in school.

It was during this time that most of the non-curricular activities took place and when we could enjoy some relaxation and relief from a regimental routine. Games of cricket, hockey, football and boxing were organised by the staff that lived with their families on the school premises. There was no obligation to take part in any of the sports and boys were free to spend their time pursuing other hobbies - the most popular of which, at the time was collecting birds' eggs and butterflies. There are a huge number of the most beautiful butterflies on this planet and India has an abundance of them. More sedentary hobbies were stamp and match-brand collecting. However, if you preferred to simply get away from it all, you could pick up a packed lunch from the dining hall after breakfast and roam the hills around the school all day – as long as you made sure that you were back in time for supper in the evening.

There were, of course, designated areas that were out of bounds, mostly to protect the local farmers from having their crops of *bhutas* (Indian corn) raided by the schoolboys. The nearby slaughterhouse, bakery and main road at the bottom of the hill were included in the ban. The cornfields were beyond and below the main road. I have to say that the boundary rules were frequently ignored, as the temptation to supplement a less-than-adequate school diet was always a strong one, resulting in frequent raids on the fields, when the corn was considered ripe enough. Matches to light a fire and roast the *bhutas* were easily obtained through one of the ancillary workers and the school bakery was also raided on more than one occasion.

Pocket money was received and administered by the class master, who issued it on Friday after lessons. Many boys could only afford toiletry essentials, which resulted in a low-level barter system and, in some cases, borrowing or even cadging. Those who had the means spent their money at the tuck shop, or on the Indian sweets and savouries from the vendors, who came from the nearby garrison town of Kassoulie to ply their trade at the school on Saturday afternoons.

Just after I had finished a spell in the infirmary with mumps, Father turned up before term's end, to take us on to our new house at Deolali and yet again I found myself in unfamiliar surroundings. I suppose this was something that the children of army families came to expect. If we made any new friends the conversation would inevitably result in a discussion about how many different places we had been posted to. The biggest shock this time was that Lavinia, Bansi and Premhassi were no longer with us; Nana told us that they wanted to go back to Moradabad. I was going to miss Premhassi! No sooner had we settled into our quarters in Deolali (which was where the unfortunate incident with the gosling, mentioned in an earlier chapter, took place) than we were packing up and moving on again. We could not have been at Deolali more than a month, if that! Mum told us that we were now going to a place where there would be lots of snow in the winter.

Murree

After a two day rail journey, we arrived in Rawalpindi and stayed in rooms at the station for the night. The next morning, we climbed aboard an army truck and began the uphill journey to Murree. Murree is situated 7,500 feet up the southern slopes of the foothills of the Himalayas and was a popular hill station with the British during the Raj. Mum, Nana and Father sat in the front of the lorry; Papa and the rest of us got in the back with all our belongings. It took the best part of a day to get up the steep, winding road to our destination and, with the exhaust fumes pouring into the open back of the truck, we all felt quite sick.

Eventually, we arrived at the army depot; some *Pahari coolies* (hill porters) were hired and we started out on foot down a steep slope. There was no proper road, only broad terraced footpaths, surfaced with crushed rock. The *Paharis* had a strange way of carrying their unbelievably heavy loads. Using a broad band of webbing, they hoisted enormous loads on their backs, by wrapping this around the burden and placing the webbing either on their foreheads or around their shoulders. Even Mum and Nana were carried on the backs of the Pahari porters in *tokras*, huge, sturdy cone-shaped baskets with seats in them. It seemed a long way down into the valley before we finally arrived at what was to be our temporary quarters, a rustic-type dwelling with a red tin roof, set half-way down a steep hill. It could best be described as a timber-built hunting lodge with a veranda facing down the slope.

There was no running water or electricity, so we used oil lamps and collected water, which had to be boiled before use, from a nearby spring. In the front of the bungalow was a narrow, level piece of land that fell away sharply without any kind of protective barrier, down into the valley, whereas, looking out of a window at the back the house, you would have to crane your neck to get even a glimpse of the sky, so steep was the upward slope behind. The approach to the bungalow was a steep, terraced path which wound from the left, as you faced the hillside. To the right was a stream, fed by a spring, the source of which was much further up the hill. A forest of very tall pine trees, harbouring an abundance of wildlife, surrounded the bungalow and the air carried a constant aroma of pine.

In the absence of servants Papa took on a new lease of life, becoming more helpful by fetching water from the spring and making sure that it was fit to drink. In the mornings he could be seen sitting on the veranda cleaning and preparing the oil lamps for the coming night. He bought himself a hiking stick and began to reconnoitre the valley in the hope of finding an excuse to get out his guns; happily there weren't many large wild animals around, only the odd jackal or hyena. There was something about the place that seemed to bring out the hunting instinct and both Theo and I wasted no time in making catapults. If we saw anything feathered or furry, and it stayed still long enough, a volley would be loosed off in its direction. Thankfully, it very seldom found its mark but, on the rare occasions that it did, I would feel remorseful and put away the 'catty' for a few days.

Not long after we had moved in, the air started to get a bit chill. Father said that we would be moving up to the hospital grounds where he worked, adding that the majority of army personnel would move down to winter quarters in Rawalpindi. The now-vacant isolation ward was to be our new home for the winter. We used only a few of the rooms in this pentagonal shaped, tin-roofed building, which was perched on a hilltop above and away from the main hospital complex. A veranda stretched three quarters of the way around the front and sides. Again, the approach was from the left and up a steep footpath. The front of the building overlooked the complex, while at the rear was the crest of the hill which fell sharply away, more than a hundred feet to the bottom of a precipice. At the bottom of this lay large quantities of discarded hospital waste: blood-stained dressings, plaster casts and general sanitary waste.

At first there were few kids of our age to make friends with, as most army families had already moved down to Rawalpindi for the winter. Those staying behind lived in the garrison quarters, which were a couple of miles away from the hospital. We managed to hire a couple of servants on a daily basis, mainly to run errands and to keep the fires burning. After settling in to our new winter home, I set out to investigate the area. There were no level roads or footpaths, which meant that, once you stepped out of the house, it was either a downhill or an uphill journey.

The area behind the isolation ward was the most spectacular, as far as I was concerned. The hill ended abruptly at the crest, almost as if it had been dissected along the ridge, with one half disintegrating onto the floor of the valley. The valley was strewn with some of largest single boulders I have ever seen, some even bigger than a house. Needless to say, my father had already declared that area out of bounds to us.

However, my enquiring nature often got the better of me and this was one of those occasions. With an uncontrollable urge to discover what was beyond the horizon, I soon found myself standing on the edge of a cliff, gazing down into the valley, lost in my boyish fantasies. Suddenly, I noticed a male figure dressed in European clothes, with a knapsack on his back. He was walking along a narrow footpath well below me and had stopped briefly to pick up a rock to hurl into the valley. Thinking that this may be an opportunity to make a new friend I copied him, by also hurling a stone into the valley. My poor judgement sent the stone short, missing him but landing a little too close for his comfort. He looked up at me, paused then shouted out, "You shouldn't do that, you know." My attempt at making a friend had fallen, quite literally, on stony ground. I wandered home, disconsolate but soon forgot about it.

The next day Papa and I were having a conversation on the veranda at the side of the house, when a familiar voice came from inside. "Where's that second-eldest son of mine?" I froze; Papa stared at me and told me that I had better go but, before I could move, Father appeared in the doorway wearing his hospital whites and with a cane in his hand. "Where were you yesterday afternoon?" he bellowed. In a state of panic, and not even knowing why I was in trouble, I said nothing but jumped off the veranda. I knew instinctively that this particular tone of voice always accompanied a beating. Unluckily, the fence protecting the side of the house prevented my escape; I was trapped. In my fear and confusion I began to shout back, "What have I done? What have I done?" By now he was on the veranda steps. "I'll tell you what you've done," he said. "You've ignored my orders to keep away from the area at the back of the hospital and what's more, you've been throwing stones at my commanding officer's son!"

I kept my distance as he stood on the steps but there was no escape route other than past him and through the house. Pointing the cane at me, he warned, "If I have to chase you, you'll get a double dose." For a moment, resignation seemed the best option and I began to walk slowly towards him. But as he stepped down off the veranda, I saw an opening appear behind him and stupidly made a dash for freedom. Unfortunately, he was a bit quicker than me and grabbed me by my shirt. My attempted escape had enraged him even more and he called out to one of the servants to get a *kursi* (chair). He knew that if he let go of me there would be another bid to escape, so the chair was placed near me and he then ordered the servant to hold me by the wrist while he unbuckled his belt. Winding it around my wrists he made me sit in the chair, legs astride and facing the back, then tied my hands behind the back of the chair and to one of the rungs. Realising that wouldn't be enough to hold me still, he shouted to the servant, "*Kuch rassi laana!* (Bring some rope!)" The servant brought what my sister has subsequently informed me was the washing line and wound it around my legs, tying them to the legs of the chair.

With a lecture on obedience, delivered in a voice loud enough to be heard all around the hospital complex, he began to bring the cane down on my back and backside. At the time I was unaware that most of the rest of the family were witnessing my punishment from the veranda. This time Papa had to stop him and I remember him saying, "Enough now, George." He grabbed Father's arm and took the cane away from him. I looked up and got a glimpse of Father's face, red with rage, eyes bulging out of their sockets.

His parting comment was, "I'm fed up with your continuous bloody disobedience. I cannot get sense into that thick skull of yours. From now on, I'm going to have to start using my fists on you."

Curiously enough, I don't remember crying very much. Papa untied me, led me into one of the bedrooms and made me lie face down on a bed. Nana sat beside me and, in the midst of a whispered conversation with Papa, she once again rubbed Germolene on the weals. In my head I tried my hardest to be rational, telling myself that it was stupid to throw stones, and my mind went back to Barnes School, where the Headmaster had given me 'six of the best' for the same offence. There had been no Nana to put Germolene on the bumps then! I also remember thinking what a sap that kid was for saying that I was throwing stones at him, when I had only thrown one and it had missed him by a mile! Later, I was to meet up with this kid again and learnt that his name was Hugh Hewlett. He was quite a lot older than me but actually turned out to be quite friendly. Once or twice he even invited me over to his house to play with his collection of Dinky toys!

Father, right & work colleague

White Christmas

One morning, we woke up to a heavy fall of snow, at least a foot deep. This is what we kids had all been waiting for! We had all been kitted out with heavy winter clothes and gumboots and couldn't wait to get out into it. This would have been the first time that any of us kids had seen snow; even Nana and Papa shared our excitement. At first, it was quite bewildering to see such a change in the landscape, with all the hospital roofs covered in a thick cushion of snow and the branches of trees shrouded and sagging under the weight. Also covered were the steep slopes of the landscape around us; it was not going to be too difficult to keep ourselves amused! I managed to pal up with some of the older kids from the garrison quarters, who had spent previous winters in Murree and had equipped themselves with good sturdy sledges. Needless to say, we spent most days discovering better and more daring slopes to sledge down.

It began snowing at regular intervals and a bulldozer was used every couple of weeks or so to keep the road clear. It became difficult for the weekly supply trucks to reach us up at the hospital, even with chains fitted to their tyres, so men with shovels and sacks would have to be on hand to help them. The snow would get piled up on the sides of the road, six feet or more high, turning the road into a single track. Walking into town and up to the Mall became so hazardous that every thirty yards or so, a recess was cut into the snow on the sides of the road, so that walkers could get out of the way of traffic.

I soon realised that having your own sledge was essential, so, with no money to buy one, I decided to build my own. I cadged a discarded wooden packing case from the ration stand and, using Papa's tools, I managed to construct what to me seemed like a half-way decent sledge. I attached the metal binding strips from the case to the bottom of the runners, in the hope that this would make it run smoother and faster. With a big smile on his face Papa said, "It looks a little flimsy," and he cautioned me about getting splinters in my behind. I was anxious to test it right away, so chose the nearest 'test track', which happened to be the path to the house. I pointed the sledge down the slope and sat on it, expecting a sudden surge of speed, but there was no movement.

Deciding that the path wasn't steep enough, I began to look around for something more challenging. I remember that the nearest suitable spot was at the back of the house. In the full knowledge that this area was out of bounds and that it may indeed be a little too hazardous, not to mention what would happen if my father found out, I decided to throw caution to the wind and proceed with a full test-run from the top of the hill and down to the cliff face away from the house. With the wild optimism of a complete amateur I decided that I would easily be able to stop before I got to the edge of the precipice. Again, at first there was no movement from the sledge. I began to bounce on it; still no movement. With frustration creeping in I began to use my feet frantically to get it to budge, when it suddenly took off and I lurched backwards. Before I managed to regain my balance I was in free fall and hurtling towards the cliff edge at an uncountable speed - too fast to even think of taking evasive action. I don't know what divine force was watching over me that day but the sledge suddenly veered to the left and capsized, throwing me off. I tumbled towards the edge of the cliff and stopped. I lay motionless on my side, afraid to make a move, not knowing how close I was to the edge of the precipice. Cautiously lifting my head, I brought my knees up to my chest and eased myself into a crawling position. I was now looking down at the floor of the valley and the hospital waste at the bottom of the cliff. A sudden loss of energy gripped me; I felt giddy and sick with fear. Gradually, I inched backwards and sat for a moment in the snow to recover. The realisation of what I had done began to sink in; I crawled back to retrieve my sledge and dragged it back towards me. Sheepishly, I made my way back and slipped quietly into the house. Later I let the servant chop it up for kindling!

For years afterwards, my blood would run cold whenever I pondered the potentially horrific consequences of that incident. Even more years later, I would have nightmares about stepping off a cliff, flapping my arms furiously in a vain attempt to stay airborne but, as the ground approached, I seemed to decelerate and land softly on my feet.

My self-inflicted ordeal must have had a disturbing affect on me at the time, as I didn't feel too well for a couple of days. Nana noticed and kept sticking a thermometer in my mouth, asking me if I felt all right. On this occasion, as nobody had witnessed this near-fatal adventure, I decided not to share my stupidity with anyone - not even Nana!

Meanwhile, Christmas was getting very close and the excitement was beginning to build. When I say 'close', I should point out that the preparations for celebrating did not commence until just a few days before the event. As there were no ready-made decorations or artificial Christmas trees, the whole family would get involved in making paper chains and blowing up the balloons ready to hang up - but not until Christmas Eve. Mum was the usual instigator, although the servants also enjoyed being involved. Getting hold of a Christmas tree was easy. You just armed yourself with an axe, selected a tree, chopped it down and then got one of the servants to drag it home. Another peculiar tradition in India was to construct a container of some sort, out of very light paper, and fill it with puffed rice, mixed with a handful of low-value coins. It would then be hung from the ceiling or a ceiling fan and, at the end of the party, one of the grown-ups would rip it open with a pole, allowing the contents to empty onto the floor. This would cause a mad stampede by all the kids to grab as many of the coins as they could find.

Christmas presents would consist of a single item each: a doll or pram for the girls, Meccano sets, or boxing gloves for the boys and bottles of whatever alcohol was available for the grown-ups. There wasn't generally much choice but I must mention that this particular Christmas would be the first time we saw a Mars bar.

On New Year's Day Father invited some of his work colleagues up to the house for a drink and a game of bridge. It was the first time that I had ever seen Papa, who was of Irish descent, become aggressive. Evidently, the one thing that upset him was losing, even at cards. As the afternoon went on the drinks flowed and Papa's voice became louder and louder. Things escalated into a fierce argument between him and one of the guests, which ended with Papa issuing threats - much to the embarrassment of Nana and Mum. Somehow they managed to subdue him and get him to bed, where he slept it off.

After the excitement of the festive season had died down, the next month passed by without much incident. We kids would amuse ourselves playing mostly outdoors during the day and sitting around a huge log fire in the evenings, listening to Nana relate family anecdotes and ghost stories.

One day, Papa suggested that we go for a hike down in the forbidden valley. Armed with a shotgun and a couple of servants (who said they knew the area well), Papa, Father, Mum, Theo and I spent the whole day in the valley but, as it turned out, we couldn't find our way back! Luckily, we came across a small village, where the head man insisted that we stayed for a cup of tea, before sending us off with one of his men to show us the way. To my great disappointment, we returned without a single shot being fired.

Back to School

Soon Theo and I were back at Sanawar. I don't know why, but we always seemed to arrive at boarding school after everybody else and leave before them. Theo was now ten and I was nine. After settling down to the usual routine of regimentation I became a little more relaxed and took up collecting butterflies. Their incredible beauty fascinated me and I made my own net from a remnant of mosquito net, some wire and a length of bamboo. I spent much of my leisure time trying to catch as many different varieties as possible. I enjoyed my own company and felt no desire to form friendships with other kids. I also became interested in sport and, while not being skilled in any particular one, I seemed to be included in any inter-house selections for cricket, hockey and football. I also visited the gym to pick up tips on boxing from the older boys, though Outram House did not field a boxing team. We were considered a little too young for competitions but, on rainy days, the older boys would get a bit of amusement by staging bouts of 'milling' between us younger ones. We would be split into two teams and lined up on diagonally opposite corners of the ring; then a boy from each corner would enter the ring and a one minute round would be started by a referee, whose only instruction to the combatants was, "I don't want to see any tears!"

It may strike any reader of my account of my time at Sanawar, that I make no mention of the academic notoriety of this educational establishment. It was indeed renowned for its high standard of academic excellence and, throughout its history, many of its pupils succeeded in becoming high-ranking officers in the armed forces, captains of industry and commerce, as well as leading members of the professions. It was also well known that, owing to the high standard of military training, it was possible for the Army to recruit boys of eighteen years old straight from the school and send them into combat.

My ability to absorb academic knowledge was severely hampered by my constant battle with the written word. These indisputable high standards meant nothing to me but the most frustrating thing was that I had no way of expressing my difficulty. Furthermore, even the thought of confiding in anyone filled me with shame and embarrassment. Looking back, I was not emotionally equipped to rationalise my situation at that age. Surprisingly though, this impediment went largely undetected by teachers, and even my parents. I do suspect that my father considered me to be 'educationally subnormal' and this may explain the sense of hostility and rejection I always felt from him.

My days at Sanawar seemed to be dominated by a desperate need to conceal my academic difficulties. My main tactic was to strive to be the equal of my peers in other ways, outside of the classroom. I tried to develop practical skills in sports like cricket, hockey and boxing and any of the other pastimes requiring physical skill and dexterity. But the classroom was a different matter; inevitably, my anxiety and fear of the learning process increased and I would therefore keep a very low profile. I took great care not to attract the attention of any of the teachers, for fear that they might single me out to read aloud or, even worse, chalk something up on the blackboard. It is difficult to describe; the harder I tried, the more nervous I felt. Just the thought of being under scrutiny would bring me out in uncontrollable palpitations. Luckily, for the most part, I managed to avoid such situations. Inevitably though, my luck was to run out......

Ironically, the lesson that day was Latin; so far it seemed to have escaped the teacher's notice that I wasn't even capable of writing legible English! This was all the more strange because the Latin teacher was 'Chicky' Evans, who also happened to be my English teacher. While the rest of the class were reciting Latin declensions, I was caught gazing out of a window. I became aware of an uneasy silence; turning my head back towards the class I realised, to my horror, that all eyes were looking in my direction. I felt the blood make a rapid exit from my face and I was reminded of the phrase: 'involuntary bowel action'. Chicky Evans' voice boomed across the room, "Come here boy!" With difficulty, I managed to get to my feet but, when I tried to walk, my legs turned to jelly; I felt so weak that I only just made it onto the dais, upon which Chicky's desk was mounted.

He grabbed me by my upper arm with his left hand and pulled me to his side; I momentarily lost my balance but somehow managed to regain it quickly. "Are you with us boy?" he shouted in my ear. "Yes sir!" I answered, in a voice that must have sounded like a rusty hinge on an old barn door. "Very well then, perhaps you can carry on from where the class left off." I tried to swallow but my throat had seized up and my tongue became glued to my palate. The smirks on the faces of the rest of the class didn't help much either. In a faltering voice I began, "Amo, amar, amartis, amant..." At this point, coordination between brain and lip broke down and I shuddered to a halt. Chicky Evans suddenly let go of my arm, grabbed my right ear between his finger and thumb and, with his right hand, produced a large screwdriver from the drawer of his desk. Prodding it into my ribs, he began shouting, "Come on! Come on!" I lost control of my emotions and began to cry. An uncontrollable stream of warm fluid rushed down my right leg and the class erupted with laughter. That completed the humiliation.

As my school days went on, the discomfort of having to sit in a classroom for the best part of each day, with the ever-present threat of ridicule and belittlement, began to have a negative effect on me, leaving me with no interest in gaining knowledge through the written word. I developed a phobia of classrooms; they seemed to exude a sickening smell. To me, there seemed no other way forward than to feign unconcern and tolerate the scorn and ridicule of the teachers. A female teacher once brought one of her baby's bibs to class with her, tied it around my neck and made me stand outside the girls' school for the whole of the lesson. I pretended not to be bothered, by keeping a fixed grin on my face. The memory of such humiliations haunted me well into adulthood.

Evacuated from School

It was now August, 1947. After yet another spell in the infirmary, this time with whooping cough, I returned to barracks. The Outram boys were now wearing a strange new uniform: grey shorts and light blue shirts, grey long socks and a military type side-cap. The uniform may have become more relaxed in appearance but the regimental discipline remained unchanged. The talk was all about the forthcoming visit to the school by the Viceroy, Lord Louis Mountbatten, who was in India to oversee the transition of British Government rule to the Indian Government and was to visit Sanawar while he was in Simla. A big parade was organised in his honour, which I missed, owing to my illness.

In the weeks following the parade, the older boys began to report incidents of shouting and screaming coming from the road in the valley below the school. I was too young to understand any of the politics of the time but later I was to learn that this was the start of a mass exodus of Muslims, attempting to leave India for the safety of the newly-partitioned area called 'Pakistan'. At the same time, those Hindus who found themselves trapped on the 'wrong' side of the border were forced to run the gauntlet in the opposite direction. Atrocities of unbelievable proportion were now the order of the day. For months, railway stations and roads were littered with rotting corpses, both human and animal. Towns and villages bore the scars of burnt-out businesses and dwellings. Though I didn't personally witness any of these horrific, murderous acts, the visible aftermath left little to the imagination.

September arrived and it was time to go home. Theo and I were surprised to see Papa arrive to accompany us home instead of Father. He brought with him some 'civvy' clothes, which turned out to be much too big, as the school had sent my parents the wrong measurements for both of us! Papa explained that we now lived in a place called Quetta, which was across the new border in the newly-formed part of the country called Pakistan. With no understanding of the situation we were nevertheless excited to be going home. Papa told us that the Government had hurriedly made emergency arrangements to evacuate all Hill School pupils whose homes and schools were now on opposite sides of the new border. He added that we were to have a military escort. We marched down to catch the toy train (it was always a treat to ride on this miniature railway) to Kalka.

On arrival at Kalka, the excitement began to grow. The sight of British and Gurkha soldiers in their trucks, waiting to escort us in a convoy of civilian lorries, added to the tension. Being too young to realise the gravity of the situation, it all seemed quite thrilling. In fact, the escalating lawlessness throughout the country had made it far too dangerous for anyone to travel on the rail and road systems.

The plan was to travel all day and lay up at pre-arranged safe places for the night. At the same time, we would rendezvous with convoys from other schools, either going in the opposite direction to us, or merging with our convoy. I'm not sure how long this journey took, but I imagine that it must have been the best part of three days. The main objective of the exercise was to deliver vulnerable school children safely across the new, somewhat imprecise borders. No provision had been made for comfort or fine dining and, while on the road, it was a matter of 'every man for himself'. Finding a spot on the floor of the packed lorry was difficult enough at the best of times. At night, conditions were so cramped that it was impossible to stretch your legs or get any sleep. If you moved an inch the space would soon be filled by someone else's body part.

During the day the diet on the road was hard-boiled eggs, with bread and water but, on overnight stops, we were treated to cooked food provided by the Red Cross and local volunteers. It was then hard boiled eggs and hot tea for breakfast in the morning, before setting out again.

The opportunity to attend a call of nature came only during the infrequent stops, which were made while the advance party went off to check that the road ahead was safe for us to continue. The armed soldiers would alight from their vehicles and line both sides of the road, before allowing anyone else off. There were a couple of occasions, closer to the border areas, when we were ordered to lie flat on the floor of the lorry. This caused some mild concern, but I suppose that the greater hazards were the lack of sleep and hygiene. Naturally, 'numb bum' syndrome was also a problem!

The journey ended in Lahore, at a place called The Burt Institute. Auntie Doris and Uncle Malcolm Skilling were there to greet us - we had not seen Auntie Doris since I was about five years old. Uncle Malcolm was now a Captain in the Army Catering Corps and lived in a large house within the cantonment area of Lahore. They took us to their home by car; Auntie Doris arranged for us to have a hot bath and we ate the first meal we had eaten in comfort for three days. She also had our clothes taken away and washed. As these were the only sets of clothes we possessed, both Theo and I had to knock around the next day wearing some of my cousin Leonard's old shorts and shirts. Leonard was about sixteen years old and we were only nine and ten. I remember having to hold on to the waistband of my shorts to keep them up, while walking around the Skilling's huge garden. We only stayed with them for a couple of days before we caught another train, this time to Quetta.

Quetta 1947

Quetta, the capital city of Baluchistan, was (and still is) isolated from other major Pakistani cities. The closest city was the seaport of Karachi, 366 miles to the south. Rawalpindi was 424 miles to the northeast, with Lahore about 445 miles to the east. Before Independence was declared in 1947, Quetta had been a garrison town which the British Government had purchased from the Khan of Kalat back in 1876. With Iran to its southwest and Afghanistan to its northwest, Quetta became absorbed into Pakistan during the process of partition.

It was home to the British Army Staff College, an Officer training facility, and today it still performs the same function for the Government of Pakistan. Over the centuries it was fought over by the Moguls and the Khans of Kalat and, in the early 7th century, was ruled by the Persians.

The usual practice, when the British acquired strategic towns and cities in India, was to divide them into sectors. The more rural and less crowded areas were dominated by the British Army and attendant families, and were designated the cantonment area. The rest was left to the indigenous population and called the city area. Often, these were served by separate railway stations and many places in the subcontinent, for example Lahore and Bangalore, still have 'twin' stations, suffixed by the words 'Cantonment' or 'City' respectively.

Quetta has always been regarded as a 'wild' border town - and remains so to the present day. The population consists of diverse ethnic tribes, many of whom lay claim to the title 'Khan'. That is, they believe that they are warriors, descending from the time of Genghis Khan. We would come to refer to them as 'Pathans'.

In the late 1940s and early 1950s it was a common sight to see the various Afghan tribesmen, decked out in their traditional costumes, when we were out on family trips to the bazaar or town. Invariably, their outfits would be accessorised with long-barrelled, locally-manufactured rifles, slung over their shoulders. Their upper bodies would be decorated with criss-crossed bandoliers of ammunition, worn like male jewellery - or perhaps, a show of defiance to those who may not quite agree with their views. That would probably have included the British rulers at the time.

On the day we finally arrived at Quetta both Mum and Father were at the station to greet us. I hardly recognised either of them. Father, who had always been on the skinny side, was now only half the man he had been. Mum also seemed to have lost weight. In the *tonga*, on the way to the married quarters, I had to keep looking at both of them to convince myself there was no mistake. After settling in and familiarising myself with the new surroundings, I noticed some new servants: an *ayah*, a cook and a teenage girl instead of the usual houseboy. Ever since we had left Lavinia, Bansi and Premhassi back in Meerut, we had had several sets of servants but I hadn't been as familiar with them as I was with the first three. I can't even remember any of their names.

For the first six months or so, the movement for Europeans, Anglo-Indians or anyone of a Christian persuasion outside the cantonment area was not recommended, owing to the continuing bad relations between opposing religious factions. Our servants, being Christian, were naturally reluctant to go anywhere near the town to pick up any groceries or household items we may have needed. Fortunately, army personnel were issued with a ration of staple foodstuffs, which would be collected on a regular basis from what we called the 'Ration Stand'.

A servant would be sent to the Quartermaster stores with a note, stating the name, number, and rank of the soldier, as well as the number of dependants, and would return with appropriate quantities of flour, rice, sugar, tinned meats, vegetables and the hated tins of margarine. There were also some carefully-vetted vendors of essential produce - fresh fruit, vegetables, meat and bakery items - who were permitted to ply their trade among the barracks and married quarters. The army also had its own dairy, which delivered milk and other dairy products on a daily basis.

Meat had to be purchased and eaten on the same day or, at the very latest, the following day and the same applied to most milk and dairy products. Refrigerators were unheard of at the time, though there was a quaint piece of household furniture called a *dooley* (meat-safe). All homes were equipped with one of these wooden-framed cabinets with a fly screen and metal mesh panels. Nana was the custodian of this piece of equipment. The *dooley* could be hung from the ceiling, placed in the larder, or stood on the floor, with its feet placed in earthenware bowls of water to prevent ants, termites and other insects from climbing up and entering the cabinet. Nana also used it for setting her *tyre* (yoghurt).

In 1948, I was in my tenth year and it was now the period of transition from British to Indian rule. It became increasingly uncertain which, if any, of the previously British-run schools would be available to us after the transition. This meant an extended holiday for many school-aged children living in the newly-partitioned areas of India and Pakistan. Unaccustomed to so much free time, we nevertheless found ways to amuse ourselves. Apart from the usual impromptu games of cricket, hockey and football - played on any available surface - there were other games we enjoyed that required no special equipment, just a little imagination. These included games like Seven Tiles, Kick the Can and *Gilli Danda*. To the uninitiated these three will need some explaining, which I will attempt to do in the next chapter.

Fun and Games

The only equipment needed for the game of Seven Tiles was an old tennis ball and seven pieces of either broken flat roof tiles or similar-weighted material, which were broken up to form a graduated stack of seven pieces, like a pyramid. The stack was then placed in a circle about four feet in diameter, drawn in the dust. Two lines were also made in the dust, ten paces either side of the circle. The participants were divided into two teams and, following the toss of a coin to decide who was to be the attacking side, both sides would retreat behind their respective lines. The objective of the attacking side was to throw the ball at the stack of tiles, in order to knock them over, each team member taking three turns. If no-one was successful in this, the opposing team would then become the attacking side. Once the tiles were knocked over, the attacking side would scatter in all directions, to avoid being hit with the ball by the defending side, while attempting to rebuild the stack of tiles in their correct order. Should they be successful in rebuilding the stack of tiles and avoiding being hit by the ball, they would claim victory and earn a second innings. However, should anyone of their side be hit by the ball at any time, the other side would take over the attack.

Kick The Can may be familiar to many of you, especially those of an older generation. It was played in a similar manner to hide-and-seek, but with the added excitement of placing an empty can in a circle. With the 'Eenie, meenie, minie, mo' process of elimination, a pursuer would be picked. He or she would cover their eyes and place one foot on the can, while counting to one hundred, after which he or she would try to find the hiding place of the others. Once spotted, their name was called and there would then be a race between pursuers and pursued to be the first to 'kick the can'. If the pursued got there first, he would be home, safe. If not, he would be 'out'.

Gilli Danda is a little harder to explain, but let us just say that it involves two sticks: a big one, called the *danda* and a small one, called the *gilli*. The *gilli* is placed in a groove in the ground. The *danda* is used to flip the *gilli* into the air and then hit it away as far as possible. The player then has to run to reach an agreed point outside of a circle before the *gilli* is retrieved by an opponent. In a way, I suppose it is the ancestor of games like cricket and rounders. The point I am making here is that these games took little imagination and almost no apparatus, but still afforded endless hours of entertainment and fun. I cannot remember anyone ever saying they were bored because there was nothing to do.

It is often said that the best inventions can be attributed to accidental discovery. Well, it was during one of these childish games that I 'discovered' the basic principle of what was to become a fascinating hobby and later, my part-time profession. It happened while I was hiding in an empty outhouse during a game of Kick the Can. The inside was pitch black, except for a beam of light which entered from a small hole in the middle of the door, about two thirds of the way up, caused by a small knot that had fallen out of the woodwork. This created a beam of light, which was projected onto the wall opposite the door. I noticed that whenever anybody passed within a certain distance on the outside, their image would appear on the wall. It was blurry and upside down but it gave me advance warning of anyone approaching, and enough time to break cover and try to outrun them. I suppose that my thought processes were not sophisticated enough to wonder how this marvel had occurred - nor to share it with anyone else; on the contrary, I viewed it as my own secret weapon in any game of hide-and-seek! Later in life, while teaching myself photography, I came across a diagram and explanation of the basic principles of a pinhole camera. I realised that I had learnt this lesson years before!

No. 1 Lytton Road

We spent the first half of 1948 in army quarters. Then, one day a lorry arrived to load all our possessions and, as we had been through this routine many times before, none of us gave it a second thought. Within an hour, we found ourselves occupying yet another home. The difference this time was that it was within an enclosed colony of privately-rented dwellings, arranged within a quadrangle. This was surrounded by a high mud wall, built in the traditional style of the North West Frontier region. There was a single, gated entrance to the colony, with a small mosque on the left side of the gate. A community of European and Anglo-Indian civilian families occupied the eight dwellings within the colony. These were all families who had once held responsible jobs with the police, prison service, railways, army, or civil administration serving the British government. They were either on the point of being replaced by their Indian counterparts, about to retire, or in the process of making plans to emigrate to a country of their choosing.

The colony was situated at the south-western end of the town of Quetta, at the beginning of the main thoroughfare, Lytton Road which ran parallel to the main rail track. An avenue of trees separated the tarmac road from a horse track which, in the past, was used by army officers and their wives for their daily horse-riding exercise. However, it was now used mainly by camels and donkeys, transporting agricultural produce from the orchards and farms around the area. The actual address of the colony was, 'No. 1 Lytton Road'.

Other points of interest in the area were a railway level crossing, a hospital, the railway locomotive maintenance workshop and of course, a local shopping area we called the 'Chowk', from where we sourced most of our daily needs. Between the rail track and Lytton Road ran a long row of houses belonging to the rail authority, where the more senior rail-workers lived. At the time, I suppose they were the lucky ones who still had employment - but even they were living on borrowed time, as their jobs would eventually be given to Indians.

We settled into one of the end-houses and shared a courtyard with the house facing opposite. For the first couple of months we had the place to ourselves but then the Wilson family moved into the house opposite. There were two boys, one about twelve and the other about eight years old. Their father was the Superintendent of the Mach high-security jail, located in a coal-mining town several miles south of Quetta. At first things seemed fine at No. 1 Lytton Road and, as none of us were attending school, there was plenty of time to explore the new surroundings. As time passed, the excitement of becoming familiar with my new surroundings ceased to mask the fact that my father had become conspicuous by his absence…

I consulted the fount of all knowledge, Nana, who explained that Father had had to be invalided out of the Army, as he was suffering from a dreadful disease called 'tuberculosis'. She added that he was very ill and would probably have to spend a long period in hospital. "Is that why we no longer live on the camp?" I asked; she nodded the affirmative. It now dawned on me that, for the past six to eight months, Father had been very quiet and I had noticed that he was looking more and more like a skeleton. I sat quietly beside Nana and pondered the situation briefly, then asked, "Is he going to die?" Nana hesitated and then slowly turned her face to me. "I certainly hope not," she said, "but it is a very serious disease." I noticed a glint of a tear in her eyes. Swiftly, she turned her head away, took a handkerchief from her wristband and held it to her face. I had never seen Nana looking so sad before and I felt sympathy for her but unable to express it, I said nothing, got up and walked away quietly.

Hard Times

Until now the family had been reliant on the Army for most of its needs. However, towards the end of 1948, the entire proceeds from an army gratuity payment had been spent on Father's treatment. We were now confirmed civilians and our income had dropped to that of an army disability pension, supplemented with Papa's small Railway pension. It was barely adequate to sustain a family of five kids and four adults. With the added high costs of medical care for Father beginning to mount up, bills were not getting paid. The first thing to go was the electricity.

At first, the local traders and vendors were reasonably content to supply us on credit but, when we began to default, their confidence soon dwindled. However, there was one man to whom I will forever be grateful. If there is such a place as Paradise, then I hope that this angelic old man entered it in a blaze of glory. 'Dither', as we called him, was a tall, bearded, humble, old Punjabi man, who rode a rusty old bicycle with a black tin trunk strapped onto the back. He delivered bread regularly and also kept us supplied with confectionery and cakes at celebration times like Christmas, Easter and birthdays. Without question, he would accept whatever we could afford at the time and then patiently wait until we were able to pay the rest. I feel deeply ashamed and saddened to say that this saint-like old man was never fully paid up before we left India to come to the UK and I will carry that shame to my grave.

The servants, having been unpaid for several months, packed up and left, leaving Theo and I to take on the tasks of fetching water, shopping and running errands. Mum and Nana looked after the cooking and household chores, while taking care of the younger kids. Papa provided wood for cooking, looked after the oil lamps and also bought some poultry to keep us supplied with a few fresh eggs.

The furniture hire company arrived one day to take away the dining-table and chairs and the three-piece suite, leaving us with just the bare essentials like beds and a few other sticks of furniture. Mum had to sell her wedding ring, declaring, "This is the worst day of my life," then sank her face into her cupped hands in despair. We were rapidly descending from a life of relative comfort into one of unaccustomed hardship. There was an air of shame and a loss of dignity amongst the adults and I sometimes heard Mum sobbing during the night.

After a long spell in hospital Father arrived home looking like a victim of one of Hitler's horror camps. The cost of hospital treatment had become unsustainable, so the plan now was for him to stay at home but go into hospital for a couple of days every two months, in order to have the build-up of fluid removed from his lungs. Between hospital visits it was vital that steps were taken to build up his strength and Nana made sure that he was given priority treatment, by serving him the best food we could afford. Every effort was made to prevent infection spreading to other members of the family. His cutlery and crockery were kept separate from ours and sterilised with boiling water each time they were used. He was also isolated from the rest of us, in a room on his own.

One day, a familiar voice called my name; I hesitated and listened. Again the voice called out, this time louder and more powerful, and I recognised it as Father. Thinking this must indicate an improvement in his health, I went to the door of his room and asked permission to enter. "Empty my piss-pot will you?" he said. Without answering, I reached under the bed, dragged out the chamber pot and took it out to the shed at the end of the courtyard that we used as a toilet. I disposed of the contents down the drain and returned to Father's room. I replaced the pot and made for the door. "Make sure you wash your hands thoroughly now." "Yes, Father," I answered.

Father's condition continued to improve and he began to spend more time out of bed and on his feet. Nana announced, "He's on the mend now, but he'll probably never be the same again." He continued to make good progress but our burden of debt had mounted up to unmanageable proportions, with creditors calling at regular intervals, only to be told that their payment had been deferred yet again.

As Christmas 1948 approached, the hills surrounding Quetta became snow-capped and the air became decidedly chill. With no proper warm clothing available, Nana and Mum got to work unpicking old discarded woollen garments and knitting them into jumpers and socks for the family. Winter breakfasts consisted of *paratahas* (fried *chapatti*) and tea and were consumed huddled around the fire in the smoke-filled kitchen.

This Christmas, the most we could expect was a celebration meal of some sort. Our financial situation was very different from previous years, when we were always kitted out with new clothes and each of us kids received a toy. Even so, I think Theo and I may have been given some second-hand toys as presents.

On Christmas day, to our surprise, the *mullah* from the mosque at the gate knocked the door and insisted on shaking everybody's hand, wishing us, "A merry, happy Christmas up to you." This he did, with a good will to every family in the colony, providing us with some amusement at his choice of words. This quaint custom was part of the culture among the Christian communities in India, but it was unheard of for a Muslim cleric to be seen doing it!

There were other families in the colony who had similar difficulties to ours. Some had it even worse than us - like the Sass family and the Hannah children. The latter were a boy named Cecil, aged about eighteen and two girls, Suzy (about fourteen) and Gene (about ten). Their father, once a well-paid train driver on the railway, had contracted epilepsy and lost his job. With no prospect of him finding alternative employment, their destiny was already mapped out and they were forced to live in a derelict corrugated tin garage. The house to which the garage belonged was situated about three hundred yards further up Lytton Road from where we lived. It had been burnt down in the riots during the Partition and abandoned by its Hindu owners.

The Hannahs had no furniture; the children had no shoes and they lived like native Indians, sitting and sleeping on the mud floor. Their survival depended entirely on charitable handouts from missionaries and the Red Cross. When we visited them, one Christmas, they were huddled around one end of an old rotten telegraph pole, one end in the shack and the other sticking through a gaping hole of the tin wall. It had been stolen and dragged into the shack then set alight at one end for warmth. Mrs Hannah was feeding her family on *chapattis* and tea for their Christmas dinner. She was a skeletal-looking woman and, during the winter, she always wore a light, waist-length woollen jacket, pulled so tightly around her upper body with her right hand that its shape was completely distorted and the material badly frayed.

Occasionally, when the Hannahs came to visit us, Nana would somehow manage to find a little extra food, so that we were able to share a meal with them. Now, when I hear people mention the word 'poverty' I am convinced that they do not fully appreciate the true meaning of the word. The Oxford Dictionary defines it as 'The want of the necessities of life.' I have suffered and witnessed this, albeit only for a short period, and the experience has had a powerful influence on my outlook on life.

There remained a few families whose fathers still maintained their senior positions with either the railway, the police, or in senior government posts. Some even had business interests. Among these, an element of low-level snobbery persisted and they tended to avoid associating with those who had fallen on hard times. However, when these better-off ones had managed to flee the subcontinent, the snobbery amongst those who had to remain gradually eased off, as they too began to feel the pinch. They were left with no alternative but to close ranks and gain the benefit of safety in numbers. Of course, there were others who decided to stay put for reasons of advanced age or deep sentimentality. As for those who had no opportunity to escape, like the Hannahs, I cannot imagine what eventually became of them!

Our situation gradually became very similar to theirs. We were deeper in debt and forced to move to a three-room hovel at the opposite side of the gate from the mosque - quarters originally meant to house the servants of the tenants in the colony. The room closest to the gate entrance was built around the trunk of a very large tree, which formed the cornerstone and supported one of the walls facing the road. There was electricity but water had to be fetched from a standpipe, situated just outside the gate, which was intended for worshippers at the mosque. The five-times-a-day call to prayer took a little getting used to at first but after a while we hardly noticed it.

In spring 1950 Father still seemed to be making steady progress but the financial situation couldn't improve until he was well enough to look for work. The rent went unpaid and we existed from hand to mouth. Although aware of our situation, I was too young to fully appreciate the extent of the predicament. Nana kept reminding me not to upset Father, as it could "Hinder his progress," she would say. I made an effort to stay out of the way and passed the time by running errands for Nana and Mum, in-between times playing marbles with *chokaras*. I learnt to make and fly my own kites and got involved in kite-fighting. I began to make my own *manga* (heavy-gauge thread) which, for the first thirty feet or so of thread nearest to the kite, was covered in a mixture of resin and powdered glass. Its function was to cut the line of the opposing kite. Such pastimes began to bring me into conflict with many of the *chokaras*. They also had the effect of increasing my Urdu vocabulary, most of which could not be repeated in decent company!

The Garden of Eden

Aside from these competitive games, I led a largely solitary existence at this time. I enjoyed my own company and, armed with an improved and somewhat deadly catapult, I spent much of my time perfecting my aim.

One day I set out to explore further away from home and followed the railway tracks. I had no idea how far away from base I was heading but knew that all I had to do was to use the same tracks as a guide, in order to find my way home. After walking for about a couple of miles, I looked through a break in a mud wall on the other side of the track and saw what looked like an oasis. There were plants and flowers, neatly laid out in cultivated beds and divided by gravel paths; better still, I could see a large pool of water, right in the middle. From where I was standing I imagined the water to be at least chest deep. It looked like paradise. With so many varieties of flowers there were bound to be butterflies and I thought that this could be an opportunity to rediscover my hobby of collecting them. The place seemed to be deserted, so I plucked up my courage and entered the grounds. As I walked around I recognised many common varieties of butterfly and began to look intently for the rarer species, which I was sure must be amongst the forest of flowers.

I was so carried away with my thoughts that I didn't hear anyone approaching. A voice said, "Hello." I turned around to see a man with a clipboard in his hand. "Vut arrr you doing?" he said, in a pronounced Indian accent. Caught unawares, all I could think to say was, "Is this your garden?" "This is The Agricultural Experimental Station of the Government of Baluchista," he answered. His English was as bad as my Urdu, but a short conversation, half-English and half-Urdu, ensued whereby I explained how I came across the place and told him of my interest in collecting butterflies. At this his eyes lit up and a broad grin appeared across his face.

He invited me to see the station's collection of butterflies and took me along to the main Experimental and Entomology Laboratory building, where I was treated to the sight of a staggering variety of butterflies, moths and thousands of insects, most of which were completely unknown to me. I asked if I would be allowed to come and catch butterflies and, gently jerking his head from side to side, in the manner common only to the folk of India, he said, "Oh yus." But having spotted part of my catapult sticking out of my pocket he cautioned me not to use it within the grounds. I then got cheeky and asked if I could swim in the pool - to which he explained that it wasn't a swimming pool but an irrigation reservoir for watering the plants. Nevertheless he agreed that I could use it for swimming.

Thereafter, I spent many idyllic days at the pool and even learnt to swim on my own - wearing just my everyday shorts, which would be practically dry by the time I had worn them home.

Around this time I struck up a friendship with Trevor Beatty, David Sass, Colin Wilson and a few other boys, whose names I have since forgotten. Occasionally, an impromptu meeting would take place with one or two of them and we would go off on a mischief-making spree: raiding the fruit orchards, or stealing rides on villagers' donkeys. We vied with each other to be the best and most daring. Of course the accuracy of one's aim with a catapult was always the subject of fierce debate. If bragging were deep water we would all have drowned in it!

Another mischief-making pastime was fighting with the *chokaras*. Their style of fighting was peculiar, as apparently nobody had ever taught them how to use their fists. This gave us a distinct advantage as in most European schools boxing was one of the principal sports. The results of these skirmishes usually ended in our favour, although occasionally they beat us back, with either sheer numbers or by resorting to throwing rocks. Accuracy with our catapults became evermore essential and we fought several rear-guard actions by aiming at the *chokaras'* feet and legs to slow them down and cover our retreat!

At home, Father tried to maintain some semblance of discipline but the TB had left him considerably weaker. While he no longer had the physical strength to administer beatings, he adopted a more psychological approach when dealing with my misdemeanours, which usually turned out to be almost as painful. He would make me sit at a table, with sheets of ruled paper, a pencil and a text book - then make me copy the book word for word. This could last for the best part of the day. When he decided that I'd had enough, he would come over, pick up the paper and begin the next stage of humiliation, calling me a 'lazy little good-for-nothing'. He would also declare that he dreaded to think what was going to become of me and that I would only ever be fit to sweep the roads.

However, I had become impervious to verbal abuse, having resigned myself to it while at boarding school. Also, now that the immediate threat of physical punishment had gone, my memories of earlier beatings also diminished and with them, my fear. Looking back, I can see that I was becoming much bolder and more adventurous. My confidence had grown and I was able to enjoy some independence. On occasions, my adventures took me far away from home and my growing command of Urdu gave me the ability to conduct simple but effective conversations with the local population.

My undeveloped sense of distance would sometimes take me many miles away. For example, I liked to venture towards the airport and, on the way there, I discovered a cool stream, which ran under a bridge. I would sit on the bank and watch small fish swimming, then take off my shoes and go for a paddle. I was later to discover that this was the route Papa used to take in order to replenish our poultry stock at a farm on Quarry Road, a little further on from the bridge.

One day, a rather distinguished-looking visitor by the name of Bob Innes arrived at our house and Nana informed me that he was an old school friend of Father's. After a long conversation with Father, he left. Later that day, Father summoned Theo and me. He announced that shortly we would both be starting apprenticeships - adding that, as he was no longer able to afford to send us to school, it would keep us out of mischief and give us some pocket money at the same time. We were to start work at the Mechanical and Agricultural Cultivation Department Workshop, which was situated behind the power station at the top end of Lytton Road, inside the cantonment area. Neither of us had any idea what this entailed, or even where this place was. Later, we found out that Mr Bob Innes was in fact the Agent to the Governor General of Baluchistan. He was also responsible for other government departments, one of which was to be our new place of employment.

Meanwhile, the rent had gone unpaid for a long time and consequently we were plunged into a further change of circumstances. We were given notice to vacate the hovel opposite the mosque and forced to look for alternative shelter.

Father decided that we would squat in some derelict shacks in a compound further along Lytton Road. The compound was a scene of devastation; the grounds were overgrown with waist-high weeds and littered with burnt out wrecks of cars and lorries. The shacks were laid out in a row of single rooms. All were damaged in some way, with large holes in the walls and roofs and some had been completely burnt out. We proceeded to occupy the three least-affected rooms, with the fourth set up as a kitchen by Nana and Papa.

Nana told us later that the buildings belonged to a Hindu religious sect that had fled during the riots and that the custodian of the evacuees' property had given us permission to stay until we could find somewhere else. We considered ourselves to be lucky to have some shelter for the summer months but would need to find somewhere else to live before winter, as these flimsy structures would not be adequate for Father during the cold, Baluchistani winter.

Working Men Now!

A couple of weeks later, Theo (then aged thirteen) and myself (aged twelve) were woken up very early in the morning, given some breakfast (a cup of tea and a chapatti) and sent on our way with some vague directions. About an hour later we found ourselves approaching a heavily barb-wired compound. It was devoid of any signs but we presumed that it was what we were looking for. The presence of some large earth-moving machinery seemed to confirm this. Standing behind the gated entrance was an old *Pathan* man, his large *pagri* (turban) arranged in the typical Pathan style. As we approached he asked, "*Tu kya chaahna?* (What do you want?)" I replied in Urdu, "We are here to start work." He told us to wait; he then walked to the other end of the compound and entered a small wooden building. He returned to open the gate, just wide enough to let us squeeze through. Pointing in the direction of the small building he said, "*Whan jana.* (Go there.)"

As we walked across the yard our progress was closely followed by the workers, who remained silent, their eyes fixed on us. We entered what turned out to be part-office, part-storeroom. Behind a desk sat yet another turbaned and well turned-out Pathan man and, to his right, sat a man who I assumed to be his assistant. Initially, the Pathan looked a bit shocked at the sight of us, but he quickly regained his composure and assumed an air of authority. Without any introductions he began to question us in Urdu and, as my command of the language was somewhat better than Theo's, I did most of the talking.

He asked our names and, after some difficulty with the spelling, wrote them down in a large book and started issuing instructions. He told us that we would be working from Monday to Friday, from eight in the morning till five in the evening and that we would only be entitled to *coolies*' (labourers') wages at first, to be paid every Friday afternoon. The Pathan then sent his clerk to fetch somebody called Misthree Rahath. We learnt that, among the staff, there were Punjabi, Baluchi, Macrani, Pashtun and Farsi-speaking Afghans and that, apart from us, there were only two Christians. These were Misthree Rahath himself, who was the chief mechanic, and another chap called Michael, whose surname I cannot recall. In India the word Misthree is applied as a prefix to anyone who is considered master of his trade.

Misthree Rahath proceeded to show us around the works. On the north and west sides of the compound were rows of large, open-fronted, corrugated-tin-clad bays, each containing a huge earth-moving caterpillar tractor. Some of these beasts had metal tracks and others huge wheels, as tall as a man. All were in various stages of repair. Men in various styles of clothing could be seen working on them and one could almost identify the ethnic group they belonged to by their attire. Some of the younger Punjabis and Pakistanis went bare-headed, while the Farsi and Pashtu-speaking Afghans wore either a *safa*, (a heavy turban) or an Astrakhan hat. Others wore traditional head wear of varying shapes and sizes, arranged in a manner that signified a particular tribe or ethnic group. Almost all wore the universal *shalwar kameez*, the combination of loose cotton trousers and shirt traditionally worn throughout South Asia.

To the east of the works was the town's power station, its tall chimney stack towered above the workshop grounds, pouring black smoke. A railway line, which served both power station and workshop, ran between the two compounds; along the side of the tracks were grouped forty-gallon drums containing diesel, petrol and lubricant oils. Inside the compound were stored various pieces of agricultural machinery. To the south was the wide, double-gated entrance. At the end of our tour, Rahath said, "*Jubsa arp logue coch chatha, muge-co ow, orr poochana.* (If you need anything, come to me and ask.)" He also explained that no-one there spoke English very well but most could speak Urdu, so we would have to get used to communicating in Urdu.

It took some time to settle in. The other workers seemed suspicious of our presence and were reluctant to approach us - I suppose that they thought we might have been planted there as spies. However, as time passed they relaxed and began to engage us in conversation. This job is where I believe my true education began. I was being encouraged to get my hands dirty and to get stuck in to some seriously practical stuff. In the classroom I had been a fish out of water; here, I was in my element. Consequently, I began to gain more confidence in myself and more trust in adults. At the same time I was getting hands-on experience and knowledge of the repair and maintenance of heavy civil engineering machinery - both diesel and petrol-driven combustion engines. My Urdu also improved, to the point where I could share silly stories and jokes with the men. They would put their hands together and mimic me at prayer in church and I told them, "At least I don't stick my bum in the air and fart in other people's faces!" They enjoyed the joke!

I had begun to get on well with most of my new colleagues, but the Pathans still seemed reluctant to accept us. I found them to be a cynical, confrontational and bad-tempered race of people. Occasionally they would question our presence there, pointing out that we were only little boys, who were incapable of men's work and were taking the jobs of men. I couldn't blame them for saying so and, on occasions, it did cross my mind as to how Mr Innes had explained our presence to the management.

One day Misthree Rahath came up with the answer: apparently, Mr Innes had told him that he was concerned about the number of wasted journeys made by service mechanics, who sometimes found, on arrival at a far-away destination, that they had taken with them the wrong spare parts or oils for servicing or repairing the machines. His plan was to provide, in the shape of myself and Theo, two English-speaking boys, who would be able to read and interpret the service manuals, hence reducing such a waste of time and cost.

What struck me as odd, however, was that some of the mechanics were quite intelligent people, with enough basic knowledge of written English to qualify as mechanics in the first place. They must have managed quite well without our help before. My theory was borne out by the fact that, in the two years I was there, on only one occasion did I help one of my colleagues in such a manner!

The heavy machinery was mostly employed on Government civil engineering projects, but some of it was also rented out to large farming communities in many parts of Afghanistan and Baluchistan. As it was essential to be able to communicate with landowners in their particular dialect, most of the men chosen to operate these heavy machines were Pashtu, Baluchi or Farsi-speakers, selected for their ability to cope with the different dialects spoken throughout the region. These people were fiercely proud of their status and would not have dreamt of approaching me, 'a mere boy' for help of any kind.

Grease Monkeys

I found it quite embarrassing having to walk the length of Lytton Road to and from work, in oil-stained and greasy clothes. There were no washing facilities at work, other than a piece of cotton-waste, moistened with petrol. This would remove the worst from our hands and clothes but we still looked like a couple of grease monkeys by the end of the day. This did not go unnoticed by the European and Anglo-Indian residents who lived along our route home and I sometimes imagined I could hear them sniggering at us.

After cleaning up and changing when we got home, I would join the other kids in all sorts of games. On Fridays, what money we earned was handed over to Mum or Father but we were permitted to keep just enough to buy a cup of tea and a snack from the power station canteen during the week. If I wanted to go to the pictures I would be reluctant to ask for cash, fearing that there may not be enough to spare. I did, however, manage to persuade Father that I needed some overalls for work and I was given money to buy an old army boiler suit, which I took to the *darzi* (tailor) and had it altered to fit. The first day I wore it I felt much less embarrassed on my journeys to and from work and actually felt as if I had been promoted to the ranks of working men. To me it seemed much more acceptable to be seen in oily overalls, rather than oily street clothes!

I became friendly with a family called Holmes: Diana, the eldest, then Roger, Garth and Granville. Their father was the foreman of the railway workshops and they lived in a large house with a large front lawn, about two hundred yards up the road from us. We had to pass their house on our way to work every day. On weekends we would sometimes be invited, along with other friends of theirs, to play cricket, or some other game. It was through these social engagements that I learnt that we had all travelled in the same lorry, while being evacuated from the Hill Schools.

One day at work the gate was flung open and a strange-looking vehicle, manned by a fair-skinned man dressed in European clothes, drove into the yard. The vehicle was grey in colour and quite small, with two small wheels at the front, two much larger ones at the back and a small trailer in tow; it looked like a toy compared to even the smallest machines we had in the yard. Everybody stopped work and fixed their eyes on the strange vehicle. The driver brought it to a halt outside the office, before turning the engine off and going inside. As curious as the next person, I made my way along with some of the men to have a closer look. A short while later, the driver returned to find a small group of people inspecting the comical-looking craft. He announced, in Urdu, that he was a representative of the Ferguson Tractor Company of Coventry, England, adding, "This little machine is going to revolutionise farming in the area."

By now most of the workers had crowded around the vehicle and I was pushed to the back. The man left the front of the crowd, allowing them to satisfy their curiosity, and then came to the back and tapped me on the shoulder. He beckoned me away and offered his hand, announcing himself as Eric Thornton. He asked me what I was doing there, how old I was and why Theo and I were not at school. I told him I was twelve years old and explained our situation. He nodded his head, and said, "So, I expect that we'll be seeing more of each other." He then jumped onto the 'tractor' - for this is what it was - started the engine and left the yard.

A few weeks later, more of the little tractors begin to appear. Eric Thornton would ferry them from the railway station and park them in a corner of the workshop yard, along with some of the allied farming equipment. While I was helping one of the mechanics to assemble an engine, Eric approached me and invited me to his house for lunch at the weekend. "Bring your brother along with you," he said.

Theo declined the invitation but I turned up at Eric's place on the following Saturday, in time for lunch. Over a meal of hot curry and rice, prepared by his Burmese wife, he fired a few personal questions at me and then started to talk tractors, asking if I would be interested in learning how to operate the Ferguson tractor. Obviously, I answered in the affirmative! After lunch, he took me to the side of the house, where there were a couple of tractors parked, and got me to sit on one and start it up. He saw that I was familiar with driving theory, so he encouraged me to take it for a spin around a spare piece of ground at the back of the house, telling me to keep going around in circles but to stop and start every so often, until I became more familiar with the controls. He then left me to it and went back into the house.

After about half an hour or so he returned and signalled for me to stop. He approached with a big grin on his face, saying, "I think you'll make a very good operator, once I've finished with you." With my heart still pounding with excitement from the experience and Eric's encouraging remarks, I was bursting with pride. I said my thanks for the lunch and agreed to return on the following Saturday.

After many such sessions, I became quite familiar with the tractor and its equipment. Eric then asked if I would accompany him when he demonstrated the tractors to Baluchi and Afghan farmers. I agreed and regularly went along with him on demonstrations. He would always make a point to mention that, if small boys like me could handle the tractor, they would find it much easier. I must have been great for business but the thought of being paid never even entered my head; indeed, I never received a penny from Eric! The glory was reward enough but he did say, on a couple of occasions, that when I was old enough, he would get me a job with the Ferguson Tractor Company.

For the next few weeks, while at work and when playing games with the other kids, I made sure that everybody was well aware of my new-found status as a tractor operator. At the time, these machines were incredibly novel. Nobody had seen the like of them before - which I soon realised when people would stop and stare at me when I was driving one. The important thing to me though, was that I should be seen doing so. I grabbed every available opportunity to drive up and down Lytton Road to show off; especially when I knew that I would be seen by some of the kids that I used to play with.

I became aware that some of the men at work were beginning to have a bit more confidence in me. Even Misthree Rahath encouraged me to take on more advanced aspects of mechanics. Under the guidance of one of the more experienced mechanics, called Misthree Usuf, I became more confident at stripping down and reassembling carburettors, dynamos, water pumps and suchlike. Later on, I was even trusted with more advanced repairs, such as de-coking cylinder heads, grinding in replacement valves and replacing crankshaft bearings and piston rings. Misthree Usuf was probably in his early fifties but he looked older. He wore an Astrakhan cap and sported a handlebar moustache. His breath always had a strange smell and his eyes always seemed to be bloodshot. I had no idea at the time but I realised later that, although he was of the Muslim faith, the breath and bloodshot eyes must have been due to the effects of alcohol!

One day one of the plant operators called out and beckoned me over. I had never liked this man. He was a fair-skinned, blue-eyed Farsi speaker, but also spoke some Urdu. He had an arrogant attitude and was full of his own self-importance, always questioning why Theo and I had been employed there. He was in the company of a group of other Pashtun men. At first I thought he was going to order me to fetch tea from the canteen. I was preparing to make some excuse to refuse when, to my surprise, he began saying that someone from his village, Ziarat, had told him that they had seen a young '*Engraz* (English)' boy demonstrating the Ferguson tractor and equipment near their village and asked if it was me. I answered that it probably was, because I sometimes helped the '*Engrazie*' man on weekends. He then went on to say something to the other men in Farsi, stood up, put his hand on my shoulder and said, "*Sharbash chotar sahib.* (Well done little sir.)" With big grins on their faces, the other men also joined in the praise saying, "*Sharbash.* (Well done.)" Compliments or praise of any kind from the mouths of these Pashtun's was very rare but, at that moment, I was in danger of drowning in pride.

Tribal Life

In May 1950 an addition to the family arrived, in the shape of brother Owen. Thankfully Father had now recovered enough to look for some work and he had managed to find employment, initially on a part-time basis, as a clerk and typist with the Daga Seed Company. The boss soon began to appreciate the value of Father's superior command of English and adept typing and offered him permanent employment. The money wasn't much but with it came a company house. The house was situated almost opposite the Agricultural Experimental Station in the Sariab road and close to Father's work premises

The move took us away from Lytton Road and into a more rural environment, where there were no Europeans or Anglo-Indians. It was sparsely populated by a diverse mixture of tribes and even a rich Arab family, who lived in a big house on the opposite side of the road from us. This family had the only safe drinking water supply within easy reach and were generous enough to let us have full use of their standpipe.

Living among our new neighbours presented no real problems and, while the architecture of these dwellings left much to be desired, they were reasonably functional. The house, despite its rural location, was small but brick built and infinitely better than our previous accommodation. There were three usable rooms set in a row along one side of the courtyard, with separate cooking and toilet areas. The building, on both left and right side, was attached to a storage barn, which the seed company used for stacking tins and packing containers. We settled in and life seemed to be feeling a bit better - until one day, when Theo's pet dog, Trixie, bit him on the hand.

Trixie was by nature a very placid dog and Theo was devoted to her. At first, we couldn't understand why she would do that but Father suspected rabies and had her isolated in the barn. The next day the full signs of rabies began to appear and she died a few days later. Although no symptoms appeared, Theo had to have immediate treatment and underwent 48 injections in his stomach, given over a 28-day period. Theo was heartbroken at the death of Trixie but very lucky to get away without being infected with rabies!

Having barely recovered from his ordeal Theo then spotted a stray puppy wandering along the main road. Being soft-hearted, he decided to grab it and bring it home but unfortunately it also bit him on the hand! My father's knowledge of pathology left him in no doubt that he had to get Theo yet another course of injections. The treatment costs now doubled and placed a further burden of debt on the family finances.

A few months passed; then the boss of the seed company decided to give us the option to move into a bigger house, situated to the rear of a long block of similar properties. Here, there was ample room for four adults and six kids. The house comprised five large rooms, plus a kitchen, bathroom, wood shed and a deep well, all contained within a high-walled courtyard. While the new house was quite spacious, there was little or no furniture to put in it. There was electricity but we still had to go around to the front of the block to fetch drinking water from the Arab house. It was further away from the town but closer to the Experimental Gardens (my 'Garden of Eden'). The wide open spaces, with fruit orchards and nut trees, seemed an idyllic location for us kids and we would spend much of our time wandering around the gardens and swimming in the irrigation pond. Looking back, I suspect that these activities allowed us to forget our economic predicament.

At this point, because we didn't have servants, Theo, Barbara or I were called upon to run most of the errands. We discovered a dairy farm that supplied buffalo milk, just a short distance away, to the rear of the house, and we would make daily trips to fetch milk in a small aluminium milk churn. The house was also situated about a ten minute walk away from the small commercial area we called the Chowk. There was a butcher, a fruit and vegetable stall and a variety of other roadside shops which together served most of our daily needs.

The shop most frequented by us had to be the *dashti* (baker), where we could get freshly-baked *naans* straight from the oven at any time of the day; this was sometimes all we could afford for a daily meal. There were also bicycle repair shops, a *darzi* (tailor) and even some fast-food and Indian sweet shops, from which we were forbidden to buy anything. Although they always looked so tempting, these shops attracted clusters of flies. The danger of eating any food open to flies was something that was drummed into us time and again, as flies were (we were told) the single most dangerous threat to health. Besides, the cost of medical treatment for a large family like ours was not affordable. Whilst living here I contracted scarlet fever and I had to be isolated from the rest of the family. The only person allowed to attend to me was Mum; the concrete floor had to be washed with a strong disinfectant and Mum had to wash her hands after she had attended to my needs.

Naturally, our shopping duties brought us into direct contact with some of the local tribal people. Quite possibly many of them had never seen Europeans 'up close' before, so we attracted quite a bit of attention. While the grown-ups weren't a problem, the kids were a different matter and there were occasions when our differences resulted in conflict; hurling of insults and calling of names took place routinely. While not having full command of their particular dialects, my knowledge of the universally-understood but less complimentary Urdu phrases proved adequate ammunition to counter their insults and gibes. Mostly, these clashes led to nothing more serious than a minor scuffle but there were a couple of occasions when things turned a little more serious.

One evening, on the way back from a trip to the dairy, we were waylaid by a bunch of Pashtun *chokaras*. Theo got hit on the back of the head with a piece of hooked wire, which must have struck a blood vessel, as blood was spurting out of the back of his head. At the sight of this, the *chokaras* scattered in all directions. At first, I gave chase but stopped and turned back, as I was more concerned with the blood pumping out of Theo's head. We were not far from home and we managed to get there quickly, by which time the bleeding had almost stopped, but the back of his jacket and shirt were soaked in blood. Other similar incidents occurred while we lived among the local tribes, probably because we were strangers in their territory and it was a less secure rural area, well away from any European occupied part of the town.

Quetta was frequently shaken by some alarming earthquakes and it was here that we experienced a particularly severe one. I recall Nana bathing Ken in a tin bath and I was standing near the well talking to Papa, while he chopped kindling wood. Suddenly, the ground shook violently and the noise created by the tin roofs rattling rumbled like prolonged heavy thunder. Papa shouted out to Mum and Nana, telling them to get out of the house. He then ran in to get them out but Nana refused to leave Ken, so Papa grabbed him and dropped him out of the bathroom window onto the ground outside! The earthquake subsided very quickly and I am pleased to report that Ken suffered no ill-effects of having been thrown out of the window!

One of the most popular sports taught in most schools in India at the time was boxing. Most boys who had attended boarding schools knew the basics and were at least able to defend themselves with their fists, which gave us a huge advantage over the tribal kids. On more than one occasion, we had to take on several *chokaras* at once but it seemed so easy to run in to them and strike a few telling blows to the head and body before they knew what was happening. Once, while fighting one of them off with my fists, another managed to hurl a half brick, catching me on my right ear and splitting it open. They claimed victory and ran off congratulating themselves; to them, drawing blood meant victory. Theo was also involved in this skirmish but this time, he came out unscathed.

We enjoyed the relative luxury of our new accommodation for almost a year, when suddenly we were told that the company needed the house for one of their relatives and we had to move yet again to much smaller accommodation. This new house also faced the main Sariab road but it had the benefit of facing directly opposite the big Arab-owned house, making it easier for fetching water. Again, there were only three rooms, plus a small kitchen and a toilet in one corner of the courtyard. It was not adequate but we had no choice.

The winter of that year began early and we woke one morning to a covering of pink snow. The snow had become mixed with the red desert sand and was carried on a fierce, northerly wind from the direction of Kandahar. Theo and I were unable to get to work and the whole family spent the day in one room huddled around a small, cylindrical paraffin heater, which was the only form of heating we had. At night, every available item of clothing was thrown on top of our beds to try to keep the cold out and I remember having to walk to the Chowk to fetch some *naans* from the *dashti*. Upon my arrival, the usually open-fronted shop had a thick carpet draped across the front entrance and, as I entered, I saw many of the local people crammed inside, all wrapped in blankets or *poshteens* (long, sheepskin Afghan coats). It was probably the only warm place in the village.

We survived for a couple of days on *naans* and hot tea, sweetened with *gagrey* (molasses), until the winds relented and things began to get more bearable. Thinking back, none of us kids ever had an overcoat to wear. The only family members I can remember wearing overcoats were Father, with his army greatcoat, and Nana, with her brown woollen coat with huge buttons. Barbara says that Nana got the local tailor to make it up from a piece of blanket material. Come to think, we never had much choice of clothes anyway; Theo and I spent the winters in just a pair of shorts and a jerkin made from army blanket material. When the skin on our knuckles and knees became crusty we would rub Vaseline into them. I can't remember what Barbara, Deanna and Ken wore; Owen, only a baby at the time, probably had knitted woollen clothes to wear and was wrapped in a blanket. At the age of thirteen, I didn't take much notice of such things.

On yet another occasion, I spotted one of the *chokaras* kicking a small ball and decided to arrange a game of football with a mixture of Baluchi, Macrani and Pathan kids, a few of whom had some idea of how to play. Most, however, just thought that all they had to do was to kick the ball in any direction. With such scant knowledge of the rules the game soon developed into pushing and shoving, in an attempt to get a kick of the ball. On one occasion one of the kids grabbed my shirt and pulled me back, at which I lost my temper and let go a few punches to his head. His nose started to bleed badly; he ran away crying and the game ended. This kid lived just a few doors away from us.

We were woken the next morning to find him, his entire extended family and a number of other members of their tribe camped in front of our house. My father went out to see what all the fuss was about and was confronted by the lad's father, who held a horse whip in his hand. By then I had gone out to see what was happening and was standing beside Father. The man spoke in Pashtu so Father didn't understand a word he was saying. After a few angry-looking gestures and shouting, Father turned to me and asked if I knew what it was all about. I said that I thought it was about me giving his boy a nosebleed the day before. The man kept gesturing for me to come forward and, as I did so, he called out to his son who came and stood by his side. He pointed to his son's face and babbled on; then suddenly, he lunged forward and struck me on my left hip with his whip. I let out a yelp. Father ran forward, grabbed hold of the whip and after a short tussle, wrenched it out of the man's hand and threw it aside.

In his weakened condition, my father was in no state to tackle anyone. Luckily, the tribesman, his family and all their followers responded by leaving the scene. I was relieved but I was left with a nasty bruise on my hip. The next day Father mentioned the incident to his boss and asked if he could have time off work to report it to the police. His boss said that he was aware of what had happened, as he was also a member of that same tribe. He explained that, because I had drawn blood from the boy, it was the lad's father's tribal duty to avenge him by drawing blood from the boy's adversary. Apparently, if the incident had occurred a few decades earlier, instead of reporting it to the police, Father might have been asking for time off to bury me!

Move Yet Again

In the early spring of 1951 we received the sudden news that the Daga Seed Company were to terminate Father's employment. We were therefore forced to return to No. 1 Lytton Road, the ramshackle house opposite the mosque, with the tree in the corner. It was another decline in our circumstances but Father did manage to get a part-time job as a typist and bookkeeper with a weaving company in the town. Things seemed OK at this time, which meant that I paid little attention to family circumstances. I did notice however, that Mum was putting on weight; nothing was said until one day when I was protesting to Nana about not being allowed to buy an air gun - Nana broke the news that our finances would soon be stretched even further, as Mum was going to have another baby. Everybody else seemed to be happy with the announcement but I can't remember being overjoyed with the news!

My friendship with the Holmes kids became closer and I began to spend much of my time over at their house. Occasionally, I would accompany them to the pictures; in fact, Diana very often came to pick me up to give me a lift on the back of her bicycle. The Holmes boys and I shared a love of cowboy films, the popular star at the time being Randolph Scott. I also remember being most impressed with the film 'Journey to the Moon', which was the first 'sci-fi' film I had ever seen. The Holmes family were also friendly with a French family by the name of Pellier; Mr Pellier owned both the cinema and the ice cream parlour next door and, on one memorable occasion, I had the treat of getting free cinema AND free ice cream on the same day!

At work, I developed a friendship with a chap called Rafiq, a tall, fair-skinned, Farsi-speaking man, probably in his mid to late twenties. He worked as Mr Innes' staff car driver. He was always very clean and well turned out and wore a light brown Astrakhan cap that added to his height. Once in conversation I told him that I played 'Cowboys and Indians' with my friends at weekends. A few days later he beckoned me over and, from the boot of the staff car, pulled out what at first looked like a bent pole with a length of string attached to it. With a big grin on his face, he said in Urdu, "*Ye, meri dada aali kamaan thy.* (This was my grandfather's bow.)" He then made a loop at the loose end of the string and attached it to the other end of the pole and I saw the ancient bow take form. He explained that it had been hanging from the ceiling of his house for as long as he could remember and told me that I could keep it to play 'Cowboys and Indians' with - but added that there were no arrows to go with it!

When I got it home I set about looking for lengths of suitable material to make my own arrows. After fashioning four reasonable-looking arrow shafts, I went to the *lohaar* (blacksmith) at work to ask if he would make me some arrowheads. I gave him a piece of paper with a drawing and he told me to come and pick them up before going home. At home I found some loose poultry feathers, with which to make the flights, and then attached these and the arrowheads to the shafts. I was now ready to have some fun!

At first, I didn't have enough strength to pull on the bowstring properly, to generate enough power. However, after many days of determined practice, I was able to discharge an arrow a good thirty to forty yards. Papa saw me with the bow and arrows and enquired as to where they were obtained. I explained and he asked to have a look at the bow. Loading an arrow he then took aim at a wooden shed door about thirty yards away, pulled back the bow-string and released. The arrow found its mark, embedding itself deep in the door.

He looked down at me and shaking his head said, "I don't think you should be let loose on your own with this son, it's a lethal weapon!" The fixed grin on my face suddenly disappeared and my heart sank. "Oh hell," I thought; I had been looking forward to such a lot of fun, after all the trouble I had taken making those arrows! Papa said that he would look after the bow for me and would supervise me when I wanted to use it. He was always such a reasonable man and I reluctantly agreed with him.

However, there were those times when Papa went to Mass on Sundays and I couldn't resist sneaking out for some target practice! On one of these occasions I took a pot-shot at a large tree which stood next to the standpipe, from which we drew our water. Some chickens had been scratching around by the base of the tree and the arrow fell short, landing among the chickens, who scattered in all directions, making a terrible racket. I was horror-struck to see that the arrow had passed right through one of the chickens and pinned it to the base of the tree trunk. I panicked and started to run, still clutching the bow in my hand; after a few yards I stopped to look over my shoulder and saw that the poor chicken was still flapping its wings, trying in vain to release itself. The woman who owned the chickens heard the noise and came out of her house, yelling and screaming. She knew straight away who was responsible and came to our door with the poor bird still impaled on the arrow. She confronted Nana with threatening words and gestures and, as neither Father nor Papa were at home at the time, it was left to Nana to calm her down and agree compensation. Fortunately for me, the matter was dropped soon afterwards and I never played with the bow again.

The next big event was the arrival of the seventh addition to our family; in July 1951 another boy arrived and was named Darryl. He was home-delivered (as Owen had been), by a local midwife. For millions of Indian women home-births were the order of the day, with just the aid of a helpful relative or a self-taught friendly midwife. Hospital and doctors fees were out of the question for us at this time.

The next episode in my life in India, or should I say in Quetta, Pakistan is going to be somewhat difficult to relate. This is owing to the fact that, after a relatively quiet and settled period back in Lytton Road, events began to take a more serious turn, which was beyond my knowledge and understanding at the time. Throughout our childhood we were discouraged from joining in or listening to adult's conversations and, for this reason, I was not prepared for the life changing events that were to follow.

The Big Move

In the spring of 1952, I noticed that the adults were occasionally congregating and having long conversations in undertones. If I happened to come within earshot, they would stop; this was the unspoken signal for me to make myself scarce but naturally this would arouse my curiosity. Whenever I sensed that there was something going on, I would try to approach quietly in the hope of hearing something interesting but I failed every time! Soon there were trips to the town and the bazaars and new clothes were being bought for the family; I remember that Theo and I were each presented with a nice pair of black brogue shoes but curiously, we were not allowed to wear them. Then, on a visit to the *darzi*, long grey flannels and blazers, shirts, underwear and socks were purchased for us. All our younger siblings were being kitted out with new clothes too.

It struck me as a bit odd that we were having these new clothes so far past the Christmas period but I don't remember being unduly concerned about where the money was coming from. I suppose I took it for granted that Father was getting sufficient money from his job at the weaving factory. One day, while walking past the mosque, I noticed that the *mullah* was sitting at his shop, talking to a well-dressed Pathan man. We always referred to these ethnic Pashtun types as 'Pathans' and I had seen this particular character around on several occasions before. He was large, clean-shaven apart from a heavy black moustache and he always carried a coiled leather bull-whip in his hand or rolled up loosely over his shoulder.

I uttered the customary salutation, "*Salaam aleikum,*" at which the man pointed an outstretched arm, with palm upwards in my direction and began saying something to me in Pashto. I stopped and gestured back, indicating that I didn't understand. The *mullah* repeated the Pathan's words to me in Urdu, "*Ye aadmi boltha, 'Ke ap ka navaa kapra kaha hai?'* (This man says, 'Where are your new clothes?')"

For a moment I was silent, puzzled as to why he would be asking me such a question. The man then turned to the *mullah* and spoke to him in Pashto. Again, the *mullah* repeated what the man had said in Urdu. "He is saying your father has asked him for much money to buy new clothes for your family but you are not wearing any new clothes - why?" I just shrugged my shoulders and answered in

Urdu saying that I didn't know.

As I walked home, I mulled over what the man had said but didn't mention the incident to anybody. A few days later, I was talking to Nana by the door of the house, when the Pathan man walked by. He looked in our direction and raised his hand in a gesture of recognition. Nana acknowledged him with a nod of her head. When he had passed, I asked Nana if she knew who he was; she replied that he was a friend of the man who collected the rents and that he was a landowner and moneylender. I mentioned what he had said to me a few days earlier at the mosque. "Oh, did he?" she asked, then turned and went indoors without any further explanation. This puzzled me, as Nana was usually quite forthcoming.

A few weeks later, Theo and I were told to take a day off work and the whole family were scrubbed up and dressed in the new clothes. Two *tongas* turned up at the house and we were taken to a large building on the outskirts of the town. After alighting from the *tongas* we entered the building and were escorted to a waiting room by an Indian man. Father then went off into another room along the corridor. After what seemed like a long time, he returned and told us all to stand up, arranging us into a line in order of age. While he was doing so, an official-looking European man, dressed in a suit and holding papers, came in and greeted us with, "Good morning." We responded hesitatingly but were soon ordered to speak up by Father. After taking a good look at us, the man turned to Father, had a short conversation with him then turned to us, smiled, thanked us all for coming and left the room. We all then got back into the *tongas* for the drive back home and, after changing back out of the new clothes, Theo and I enjoyed the rest of the day off.

Although this was a highly unusual event, no-one questioned what it was all about and, although I was curious, I thought it better to say nothing. However, that evening Father called Theo and me into the house; he sat on one of the beds and told us both to sit on the bed opposite. He began by saying that, for some time, he and Mum had been concerned about the future of the family and they had decided that it would be in all our best interests to go to England, where everyone's prospects would be much better. He went on to say that he had applied to the British Government for assisted passages and explained that the trip earlier was to the British Secretariat and was to verify the number of family members making the journey. He added that things were now at a fairly advanced stage. He didn't go into any further detail but said that it was vital not to breathe a word to anyone at work or to any of our friends, stressing that a word out of place would jeopardise the whole thing.

Naturally, this news had a profound effect on me and my mind began to go into overdrive. England! What was it like? The grown-ups in the family always referred to England as 'home' but none of them had ever been there. I decided to ask Nana, who was sitting on one of the beds, combing her long hair, what it was going to be like in England. I had no idea where it was geographically but had heard of a place called London, which I knew was in England. Nana said that, although she had never been there, she had heard lots of stories about it throughout her childhood. She told me that it snowed heavily in the winter and even in the summer months it was quite cold, adding that the kind of light clothes we were used to wearing in India would not be adequate in that kind of climate. We would need to wear much warmer clothing all the time. "Like in Murree, you mean?" I said. "Yes," she replied.

Once I had started her on the subject, I couldn't stop her. She went on, "You'll have to watch your step or you'll certainly meet your match when you come up against the cockney boys. They're a rough, tough, two-fisted bunch and they won't stand for any of your lip sauce." She made an attempt at mimicking a cockney accent by saying something silly but gave up and started to laugh; I laughed along with her. I asked what a cockney was and she said that it was what they called people who lived in London. (I had thought that everyone in England lived in London!) "Mrs Conn, who lives across the way, is a cockney. Ask her, she'll tell you." I continued to throw questions at her: "How are we going to get to England and what will it be like living in London?" I listened as she rambled on about Buckingham Palace, Big Ben, 'costermongers' and street urchins. By now she had painted a picture of an exciting but complicated place to be venturing to and probably detected some concern in my questions. "Don't worry," she said, pointing to the family Sacred Heart picture that always hung on the wall; "The good Lord will take care of everything." She then twisted her long hair into a tail, coiled it at the back of her head, and pinned it in position with a hairpin - just as she always did.

I had never seen Nana lose her temper, or even become impatient, and she had always been a comfort to me in times of need. She was also a wonderful storyteller and had the singing voice of an angel. With her Victorian parlour songs and tales of the supernatural, she would keep us kids amused throughout the winter months. She had the knack of pausing at just the right moments to create tension and excitement; no matter how many times she repeated the same stories, we always enjoyed them.

I don't remember being told any further details about our intended departure and, although things must have been planned with great care and secrecy, there were no signs of clandestine behaviour from the grown-ups. One day I was passing the office at work and the clerk called out to me. He was standing in the doorway, holding an envelope. As I approached he said that Innes Sahib had told him to hand it to one of us and I noticed that it was addressed to Mr G. Smith, my Father. "Ah. I think I know what this is," said Father, when I handed him the envelope at home. He immediately opened it and, while reading the type-written contents, told me to fetch Theo. He then explained that, for our future benefit and in order to help us get work in England, he had asked Mr Innes to provide Theo and me with a written reference; there were two copies, one for each of us. I asked when we were to leave and he said that he would let us know nearer the time, reiterating that it was absolutely vital that nobody knew anything about our departure.

In the meantime, life continued quite normally, although my mind was becoming preoccupied with the need for secrecy. I would ponder it as I walked to and from work each day; why couldn't I tell my friends that I would be going to England? I also felt that I ought to say something to Eric Thornton. After all, he had said that he would get me a job with the Ferguson Tractor Company and I had rather been pinning my hopes on it. Mixed emotions began to surface in me; we had moved locations so many times before but this time it was going to be to somewhere so entirely different. The excitement at the prospect of going to England and seeing London was obvious but it was tinged with a feeling of trepidation. To make matters worse, I wasn't able to discuss my feelings with the other members of the family. In fact, there seemed to be a wall of silence on the subject.

It may have been my imagination but it seemed to me that the Pathan man, who had asked me where my new clothes were, was visiting the *mullah* more frequently. Slowly, the penny began to drop: new clothes, moneylender, going to England - was it possible that Father had asked this man for the loan of the money to finance the trip? Was that the reason for the secrecy? A feeling of unease developed in me and, if I saw the Pathan near the mosque, I would quicken my pace. I didn't want to have to answer any more awkward questions from him.

I sometimes observed Mum in her well-practised role, quietly packing the travelling trunks in-between tending to Darryl's needs. Nana, as usual, gave her a hand but there didn't seem to be any conversation going on between them that I could pick up on. Nor, for that matter, were there any other signs of the usual upheaval whenever the family were planning a move. In fact the atmosphere at home seemed fairly relaxed and it didn't seem worth working up too much anticipation by actively looking for clues. After a few weeks, with no information coming forth, I began to feel a little less anxious.

I cannot be very accurate about dates and time scales of this episode in my family's life but I would guess that it covered the period between late March and early May 1952. One Friday afternoon, I was heading towards the power station canteen, to settle my weekly bill and get a cup of tea, when my friend Rafiq drove into the yard. He stopped to say hello and asked if I would fetch him tea as well. "I'll pay you back on Monday; I haven't picked up my pay yet," he said. "You can't pay me back on Monday - I may not be here next week," I replied. He laughed and said, "*Chuloo!* (Go on!)" When I returned from the canteen, I saw Rafiq had parked his car in one of the empty bays and was wiping it clean of dust. I handed him his tea and we both sat in the car to drink and chat.

After taking a sip of tea, he said, "So! You may not be here next week. Why's that?" His question hit me like a thunderbolt. The realisation that I had let the cat out of the bag rendered me dumbstruck. There was an awkward silence. Rafiq turned his head towards me and said, "*Kia hona? Tu kuch nahin bolta.* (What's happening? You're not saying anything.)" I felt trapped, I couldn't think of an explanation for what I had said. Although I had no idea of when we would be leaving, it must have been playing on my mind and had just come out accidentally. Rafiq was no fool. He could sense my embarrassment and didn't press me any further. He quickly changed the subject and began telling me about where he had driven Mr Innes to that day. He even tried to cheer me up by telling some of his well-worn jokes, but my mind was focused on my stupid outburst and I only managed a forced smile.

For the rest of the day, my mind was completely preoccupied with my slip-up. I was annoyed with myself for being tongue-tied when Rafiq questioned me. He was bound to be suspicious now and I was afraid that he might mention it to someone else. To add to my anxiety, that same day, as Theo and I were approaching the mosque on the way home, I caught sight of the Pathan walking in our direction. As he got close, I bent down and pretended to tighten my bootlace to avoid having to speak to him. Back at home we followed the usual routine of cleaning up, changing clothes and eating our evening meal. All the while, the incident at work was playing on my mind but I couldn't bring myself to say anything to Father about it.

The Bombshell

Very early the next morning, we were woken by the grown-ups and told to get washed and dressed. We were given breakfast and told that we would be helping to put Nana and Papa's belongings on a lorry that would arrive shortly. Nana and Papa were going to live in Sariab, a railway stop several miles down the main line to Karachi. There was a sense of urgency among the adults and I realised that the secret plan was being put into action. Soon, the lorry arrived and backed up to the main gate. The tailgate was lowered and the large travelling trunks were lifted into the back, along with various other pieces of luggage. Nana got into the front with the driver and Papa climbed into the back with the luggage. As the lorry started to move off Father told all of us to wave and shout goodbye. It all happened so quickly, I don't think any of us could understand what was happening. Strangely, nobody questioned why Nana and Papa were taking all our possessions with them.

We were then told to follow the lorry out of the main gate and onto the road, still waving goodbye. We watched as the lorry went over the railway level crossing and carried on down to the Sariab road. As I turned to look at the mosque the *mullah* was setting out the wares in his shop, but I'm not sure whether he had observed the departure of Nana and Papa. Father then announced that we were all to go for a walk along the rail tracks. As we set off, it suddenly struck me that Mum and Darryl were not there, which seemed very odd; I turned and asked Father where they were and he reassured me that we would see them soon

After walking along the track at a brisk pace, for about a mile or more, we crossed over, close to the Agricultural Experiment Station and cut across through an orchard onto the Sariab road. I knew this area very well; after all, it was my favourite playground. I spotted the lorry that had just left our house, stationary on the road ahead. As we got nearer, the driver lowered the tailgate, helped us all into the back and set off. Soon, we slowed down and turned into Sariab Railway Station, just a few miles away and we all disembarked. It was then, to my surprise, that I saw Mum getting out of the front seat, while Nana was holding Darryl; they must have got into the front of the lorry before anyone had time to see them!

The luggage was carted into a waiting room, where we stayed for a while and I noticed that the adults were being strangely quiet. Some time later in the day, we boarded a train and, although Father had made no specific announcements, I knew then that we were on our way to England. As we were settling into our carriage, Mr Stilwell, a mail train driver, appeared. "Hello! What's going on here?" he said, poking his big head in the carriage door. Both Father and Papa stepped out onto the platform to speak with him. I couldn't hear what they were saying but it was obvious that they were giving him an explanation of some sort.

When they got back to the compartment and we were all together, Nana started to go around all the children kissing them and saying goodbye. This really confused me; 'What's she saying goodbye for?' I thought. The train jerked and started to move off slowly. Papa grabbed Nana by the arm and took her to the door; Father put his arms around her and was saying something I couldn't hear. It was all happening so fast; I didn't have time to think. I stuck my head out of the window just in time to see Nana and Papa walking along the platform alongside the train, Nana with a hanky to her mouth. They both drifted into the distance, as the train picked up speed. I turned to Father and asked if they were going to catch another train later. "No," came the answer. "They won't be coming with us; they wanted to stay." That was the last time I ever saw them.

These events, for which none of us had been prepared, were happening so fast that now I find it difficult to recall them in much detail. It seems to me that, a few hours after leaving my grandparents on that railway platform, we arrived in Karachi. In fact, Karachi is a day's drive from Quetta, so I can only assume that time has been compressed in my memory. At Karachi, we were taken to an army transit camp, where we stayed for a day or so. Soon after this, Owen, Ken, Deanna, Barbara, Father and I boarded a small ship, which would take us to Bombay. There weren't enough berths on board for the whole family, so it was decided that Mum, Darryl and Theo would have to go by air and join the rest of us in Bombay. On arrival, we checked into an hotel and waited for the others to meet us. Soon we were all taken to the docks by a couple of representatives from SSAFA (the Soldiers, Sailors, Airmen and Families Association – a military charity) and boarded a P&O liner called the SS Moloja. In what seemed like no time at all, we found ourselves heading out to sea and bound for England.

The last photograph taken of the family at No 1 Lytton Road
Left to right: back row - Ken, Ian, Theo, Barbara
Front row - Deanna and Owen

On Our Way to England

I have tried to cast my mind back to this momentous voyage but my memories seem shrouded in confusion. This was my first experience of a sea journey and it should have been exciting, but I can't remember being over-enthusiastic. My feelings were divided between the apprehension and uncertainty of what awaited us in England and the remorse and grief of leaving Nana and Papa behind, with the prospect of never seeing them again. I suppose, at the time, my emotional state cast a shadow over the whole event; I suspect that I may even have been suffering from mild depression. In any case, I was somehow unable to throw myself into what should have been an enjoyable experience for a teenager. Things improved slightly as the voyage progressed and eventually I began to relax a little and pay more attention to what was going on.

I seem to recall that we were all billeted on the lowest deck of the ship. As the two eldest, Theo and I were separated from the others; we slept in a four-berth cabin with a couple of older Australian Boy Scouts, who mostly ignored us. The rest of the family occupied a larger, six-berth cabin with an extra cot for baby Darryl, further down the corridor.

I recall a particular day, when the sea was a little rough and water came in through the porthole. The cabin steward had to come and secure it with brass wing nuts.

Barbara continued her role as a second mother to the younger members of the family and was continually called upon during the voyage to take care of baby Darryl. She took her meals with the younger ones in the children's dining room, while Mum and Father had their meals at a different sitting in the main dining hall. Theo and I also ate at a different sitting; we were put on a table with a lot of young, high-spirited Australians, who spent much of the time shouting silly things and throwing bread rolls at each other. My reading difficulty immediately presented me with the problem of what to order from the menu - added to which, I had never heard of most of the food listed! I generally looked to see what the other passengers were ordering before making a choice - except for lunchtime, when I always ordered curry and rice. I remember the waiter asking me if I realised that there were other things on the menu? After a while, he gave up and just brought me what I had asked for!

There was no spending money for treats of any kind, so I just occupied my time by walking around, watching the antics of the other passengers as they played deck games and ordering cool drinks from the deck stewards. I watched the other passengers' behaviour closely, as it was a novelty to be among so many white folk. I remember being quite shocked and amused at the sight of women in bikinis, sunning themselves. I had always been warned to keep out of the sun whenever possible and I simply couldn't understand why others weren't following this advice.

Sometimes, we kids would create some excitement by getting ourselves lost on the ship and then finding our way back to the starting point. At other times, I would just stand at the ship's rails to catch the cool breeze and gaze out to sea. I would become lost in my thoughts, recounting what Nana told me about the tough cockneys and wondering what London was going to be like. One thing was certain: there would be no Nana to take my troubles to or confide in.

Our first port of call was Aden. To me, it didn't look much different from any Indian town or city; if anything, it seemed even less prosperous. We left Aden and travelled the short distance to the Great Bitter Lake at the southern end of the Suez Canal, where the ship dropped anchor and had to queue for a day or more before entering the canal. From our position, anchored on the lake, the water was obscured by sand dunes and the ships sailing along the canal created a kind of mirage; what appeared to be ships sailing through the dry desert was a truly amazing sight. When we eventually entered the canal we passed by many small villages and British Army camps, from where the 'Tommies' called out and waved to us.

At the northern end of the canal we stopped at Port Said. Before we had time to dock, a number of small craft - which everyone referred to as 'bum boats' - crowded around the ship and the occupants began to throw ropes up to the passengers on deck. The ropes had baskets attached to the middle and this was their way of passing wares up to the passengers to inspect before making a purchase. When a deal was struck, the exchange of money and goods would take place via the basket. Some of the more privileged traders were allowed to come aboard and lay out their wares on the decks. There was even a magician, who entertained the passengers and passed a hat around afterwards. A few of the traders were selling brightly-coloured tee shirts and, having never seen such attire before, I set my heart on a yellow one; sadly, though, I couldn't raise the cash! I think that we must have stopped there for most of the day, as some passengers had time to go ashore to see the sights.

After leaving Port Said, the ship entered the Mediterranean Sea and there were at least a couple of uneventful days' sailing before I heard someone say, "Stromboli," at breakfast. I didn't have long to wait to discover what it meant as, a little later that morning, the decks began to fill up with people; many of them were carrying binoculars and all seemed to be in a state of excitement. I managed to find a place at the rails, just as an enormous mountain was coming into view. When we got nearer, I plucked up the courage to ask an elderly man standing next to me what it was; he explained that it was an active volcano called Stromboli and, if we had been passing during the night, we would have seen it lighting up the sky from far away. However, because it was daytime, we could only see smoke coming from the top.

After the minor excitement of Stromboli, things settled down again to the usual routine. The talk at the dinner table was about the next destination: a port called Marseille. I had never heard of this place and, the day before we arrived, I had been very late for lunch so most of the other passengers had left the table. While I was finishing my curry and rice the waiter was clearing up and asked me if I would be going ashore in Marseille. I said that I didn't know and that nobody had said anything to me about it. He told me to ask my parents to take me, as this could be a wonderful opportunity to visit the South of France. He added that it would also give me my first sight of Europe.

We approached the harbour late in the day. On first sight, it did not appear to be very remarkable and was littered with half-submerged shipwrecks. It was not until after breakfast the following morning that people began to disembark. My recollection of Marseille is, to say the least, sketchy. I don't know who I went with, or how I got there but I can remember standing in what to me seemed a very clean, almost pristine, street market; its stalls displayed huge bunches of beautiful flowers, tempting fruits and mouth-watering confectionery. The streets and houses were so clean and tidy compared to what we were used to in India. On the way back I remember walking past a shipwreck, where some workmen were dismantling the hull with an acetylene torch. One of the men said something to me in French then offered me a grimy-looking rubber doll and uttered the word, "Souvenir?"; I declined the offer!

The next point of interest during the voyage was when we passed through the Straits of Gibraltar. My knowledge of geography was nil, so the significance of it was wasted on me at the time; all I remember was that I could see land on both sides of the ship. About a day or so later the temperature dropped, the sky turned grey and the sea became rough; we had apparently entered the Bay of Biscay. While some people still walked about on deck in their customary light clothes, others had changed into warmer attire and stayed in the lounges, playing cards or board games. The talk at the dining table began to centre on various parties making pacts to 'keep in touch' when they 'got settled in' and exchanging scraps of paper with names and addresses written on them.

Then, one morning, after about two weeks at sea, the excitement really began to build. After passing a lighthouse I heard someone say that we would soon be seeing the White Cliffs of Dover. I remembered these words being sung so many times in the past but I had no real concept of their significance. Now I was actually going to see them for myself!

At lunch that day, you could have cut through the anticipation with a knife. Passengers and waiters all seemed to be talking in raised voices and laughing and joking with each other. People began to leave the table in a hurry. I stayed to finish my meal but the waiter said, "If you want to see the White Cliffs of Dover, you'd better be quick - we will be passing them very soon." I quickly finished my meal and hurried to the upper deck; it was already crowded and I couldn't find an unrestricted view, so I made my way to the rear of the ship, where there seemed to be fewer people. I climbed up onto some wooden life rafts, where I managed to get a better sight of the Cliffs. My only previous knowledge of this iconic landmark had come from the 'Tommies' playing Vera Lynn records in the barracks, back in Meerut. I don't know what I expected to see, as I looked on them for the first time, but I think that, by this time, I had had so many new experiences and discoveries in such a short period, that my young mind was quite overwhelmed!

A short time later, the ship slowed down and dropped anchor. We stayed at anchor all night and I hardly slept, with the anticipation of what was coming next. In the morning, I got up very early, dressed and went straight up on deck to get a look at England. The crew were still washing down the decks and it seemed very cold. Through the early morning fog I could just make out what appeared to be land. After walking around the deck a couple of times, I decided that there was nothing more to be seen and went back down to the cabin for breakfast. Soon after this, the ship began to move and before long we were entering into Tilbury Docks.

We've Arrived

I was on deck as we arrived and I watched the docking process with great fascination. One of the first things that caught my eye was the small ferryboats, crisscrossing the river. Many of the men seemed to be dressed in mackintoshes; they all wore funny-looking caps and hats, as did the people on the dockside.

Most of the smartly-dressed men seemed to be wearing black dome-shaped hats but the scruffy-looking ones wore flat caps with a peak; many of them seemed to be wearing a tie of some sort. It was so strange to see white-faced people doing the kind of work that, only a few weeks ago, we would have expected to see an Indian man doing - except that these men were using handcarts to carry the luggage and not carrying heavy loads on their heads, like Indian porters. The SSAFA representatives came aboard to welcome us and, when we disembarked, they helped to put us on a train; the English trains looked much bigger than the toy train we used to travel to school on in India. Along the way, my face was glued to the window; I was puzzled to see so many long rows of houses strung together with funny-looking chimney pots sticking out of them.

It was probably early afternoon when we arrived at Earl's Court by taxi and were taken to a house: 23, York Street, Nevern Square, Earl's Court, London, W1. The family were shown into separate rooms. Theo and I shared a bed in a cellar bedroom and I remember the bed being very high and covered with a patchwork quilt - the first one I had ever seen. At breakfast the next morning, we were given kippers, which I had never seen or heard of in my life! Apart from choking on the hair-like bones, the taste repeated on me all day; it reminded me of cod-liver oil. I had never been very keen on any kind of fish but I remember thinking that I would never be able to face another kipper ever again!

The house was run by a couple of kind ladies who took good care of us and made sure that we were kept busy. They prepared packed lunches for us each day and gave us maps and instructions on how to get to all the places of interest, including the nearby museums in Kensington; however, what caught my imagination most was riding on the tube trains!

The details of what occurred in the following days and weeks are again masked by what I can only describe as 'culture-shock'. For someone born and raised under 'third-world' conditions, to be thrust into a world famous modern city like London was, to say the least, bewildering. It was an assault on all my senses. My concept of the world was being turned on its head within a few short weeks, each day bringing a deluge of new experiences. Above all, I had not been prepared for the sight of all the bomb damage left by the war; it was nothing like I had imagined, leaning on the ship's rails during my voyage - nor even anything like the picture Nana had painted for me. I began to doubt my father's wisdom in bringing us to England, feeling that I had too much to learn in such a short space of time. One particular difficulty (having no experience or concept of a modern road system) was finding my way around the city; I constantly relied on directions from policemen, or even complete strangers. Getting used to the strange accents and the foreign currency left little time to commit any detail to memory. My famous sense of adventure was now diverted in so many directions that I felt ill at ease.

The ladies at the SSAFA house looked after us as a family for about a month, while Father, with no recognised employment history or skill to offer, tried to find work. With only his small army pension for an income, his lack of employment and accommodation, together with the emotional trauma of leaving his mother and the land of his birth, everything began to take its toll on him. His psychological condition worsened and one day, to everyone's bewilderment, he disappeared without trace! After making extensive enquiries the SSAFA people assumed that he had abandoned the family and, a week or so later, they took the decision to move us to a workhouse in Archway, North London.

The Workhouse

Our family then found ourselves in a large, Victorian building adjacent to an old people's home, along with other families in a similar predicament. Our accommodation consisted of what had once been a very large hall, now divided into compartments or small rooms. Mum, Barbara and the younger children were given one of these sparsely-furnished rooms, while Theo and I had to sleep in a dormitory with old men and a couple of other similar-aged boys. During the day, we were permitted to join the rest of the family for meals, etc.

A team of social workers visited Mum regularly, to assess our needs and make her aware of what benefits she was eligible to claim. She was also given advice on registering with all the appropriate agencies, such as HMRC, an NHS doctor and the Local Education Authority; I imagine this must have been a great help and relief to Mum at the time. In return, she was expected to work as a cleaner in the old people's home next door. Each day, she would take her standard issue metal bucket and a mop and join all the other mothers in a cleaning party.

I will never understand how Mum managed to take care of seven kids and do a full day's work as well. She never once complained, though I remember her sitting on one of the beds one day, with her head in her hands, tears seeping through her fingers. In times past, Mum's daily routine had consisted of issuing orders to the servants in the morning, playing badminton in the afternoon and holding bridge and whist parties on the veranda in the evening. Now, she was being subjected to menial duties - having to mop the dirt from floors. An angel had fallen from grace!

New School

The school leaving age in England at the time was fifteen and Theo, who was already fifteen, got himself a job in a local garage. Those of us who were of school age were enrolled in local schools; I attended a Secondary Modern School for boys, which was within walking distance of the workhouse. Nana's description of life in London had started to become a reality! On my first day a teacher collected me from the Headmaster's office and led me into a classroom containing about twenty-five boys. He invited me to tell the class my name, and then followed this by saying, "Ian has come all the way from India, to teach you people some manners." The words had hardly left his mouth when a voice from the back of the class said, "Sir, if 'ee's from India, why ain't 'ee black?" The teacher retorted, "Because unlike you, he washed his face before coming to school this morning!"

The class burst into uncontrollable laughter. The teacher shouted out, "All right, all right! It wasn't that funny, now shut up." He then told me to find an empty desk and sit down. Making my way through double-seated desks and loud murmurings, I could feel every pair of eyes following me; voices came from every direction, urging me to sit by them. I felt a hand grab my arm and pull me towards a seat. "'Ere mate, sit 'ere." Without much thought, I sat down. The teacher's voice boomed out, "No, don't sit near that idiot - you'll become contaminated!" An exchange of words took place between the boy and the teacher, in which the boy used foul language under his breath. I then looked for another vacant seat. I could never have imagined such unruly behaviour or bad language being tolerated in any school in India.

For the next few days I was popular with some of the kids, who seemed eager to be friendly. It was only outside the classroom, during break-times, that I got to experience the broader situation. Nana was right about the cockney accent and the bad behaviour. At first I felt a bit intimidated but within a few days (apart from the foul language) it seemed much the same as other schools I had attended. Some of the boys even tried to get me interested in their spare time activities, like Army Cadets, Air Cadets and Boy Scouts - none of which I had ever heard of - and they all seemed to be very interested in the camping side of these activities.

I was settling in nicely but, as in all schools, there were the school yard bullies and this place seemed to have more than its fair share of them. Up until now, I had avoided their attention but, during one morning break, a kid I had made friends with was standing in a corner of the playground surrounded by a group of boys. He looked to be in a distressed state. Apparently, one of the more infamous bullies had ripped his blazer pocket, while relieving him of his pocket money. He seemed more concerned about having to explain the torn pocket to his father than the loss of his money. "He'll never believe me," he kept saying. I had a fellow feeling for him...

During the following dinner break, I went over to talk to this kid to offer my sympathies. There were others doing the same and I listened for a while. I couldn't think of anything to say, other than to fall back on my father's counsel to me when I was at boarding school. I found myself announcing, "The best way to deal with bullies is to pick a fight with them, to show them that you're not afraid." There was a moment of stunned silence. Then a voice chirped up, "Oh yeah? Let's see you do it then mate." Another moment of silence followed, then another voice echoed, "Yeah – let's see you!"

I then realised that my big mouth had beaten my tiny brain in a race to the losing post; I had really put my foot in it! The familiar feelings of nausea and constipation of thought followed as I looked at their expressionless faces. I got the feeling they expected an immediate response. I paused, then the words dribbled reluctantly from my lips, "Someone's going to have to back me up, then." After a long silence, the boy who had first issued the challenge said, "Ok! I'm with you." Then another said, "Me too." Everyone else stayed silent. I was now committed up to the hilt and the only way to redeem the situation was to carry out the act of reluctant heroism.

So, during afternoon break, I went looking for my two henchmen but they were nowhere to be seen. I had no idea what this bully looked like, so I needed them to point him out; that way, I could make my assessment as to how big a mistake I had made! I scanned the faces in the yard, trying to guess which one was my target. There were quite a few tough-looking kids that I definitely wouldn't have chosen to tangle with. I leaned against a wall and waited till I caught sight of the two boys. There were some others kicking an old tennis ball around nearby and they looked every bit the kind of kids that Nana had described to me. The ball came my way and I picked it up nervously, grinned and threw it back. The scruffiest-looking one said, "Wassa matta, mate? Can't you kick a ball then?" "Not with my new shoes on," I replied - I was wearing my new brogues. He and some of his mates came up to me. "You gotta funny voice, ain't yer?" He began to mock and make fun of me. Suddenly, he pushed me against the wall, held me there and stamped on my foot, saying, "Oh, look what's happened to your nice new shoes now!"

His mistake was to stand back and start laughing. Even as the others all joined in, I launched myself at him and began to rain blows to his body and head. Some missed but some got home and he doubled up; I didn't stop. He covered his face with both hands but I kept giving him upper cuts. He turned away from me, so I pushed him to the ground, then stood over him, waiting for him to get up. It felt just like the fights I had got into with the *chokaras,* back in Quetta. The deafening noise from the crowd that had gathered around alerted the school caretaker, who dragged us apart and ordered us to go and stand outside the Headmaster's office. I led the way, slightly nervous but mostly triumphant, as I always was after winning a fight. The caretaker stuck his head round the Headmaster's door; "These two were fighting in the playground." We were called in and given a lecture, before being told that the incident would go down on our school reports. He then ordered us back to class. As we left the office the kid said, "You wait, I'll get you outside school." I didn't flinch. "Just try," I replied.

When I got to my class the teacher asked me why I was late and where I had been. As I was explaining, one of the kids in the class shouted, "Sir, he done Chalky White in." The teacher told me to sit down. As I made my way to my desk, the other kids began to say things to me like, "Smiffy, you gave it to him!" "I'm going be your mate for life!" Later, I was to learn that I had tangled with one of the school bullies all right - just not the particular one I had volunteered to pick a fight with!

That day, after school had finished, I was making my way back to the workhouse when one of the older boys caught up with me. "Chalky White ain't gonna wanna forget it, you know," - adding that Chalky's dad delivered coal to the school and, whenever he was around, Chalky would start showing off to impress him.

As it happened, I was to receive no further trouble from Chalky but, during the days that followed our contretemps, I was more careful about whom I mixed with and I kept a lower profile while in the playground. However, the older boy who had given me the warning about Chalky initiated a friendship with me; his name was Ralph. He wanted to know about my previous life and said that his uncle had served in the Army in India. One day, he said his mum had agreed that he could invite me to tea, and asked me if I had ever seen a television. Of course, I accepted the invitation eagerly; I knew televisions existed but I had never actually seen one! In the event it was a bit of an anti-climax; the screen was very small and the picture kept distorting, meaning that Ralph's dad had to keep adjusting the aerial.

Next, Ralph invited me to go along to his Boy Scouts' meeting with him one evening, to see if I would like to join. After my initial visit, the Scout Leader invited me to go along with the troop for a weekend of camping in Hertfordshire. This entailed a short trip by train and then a long walk to where there was a proper wooden Scout hut. It wasn't the most exciting weekend I had ever had; the camp activities seemed to consist of little more than cooking sausages and baked beans and then snacking on bread and jam!

Back at school, news of the Chalky White incident had spread and, while I was enjoying a degree of popularity with my classmates, the teacher was becoming concerned about my lack of commitment in the classroom. He told me that my work was very much below standard and, if I didn't show improvement before the end of term, he would have to recommend that I go down a class; this would mean being taught with much younger boys. He asked me which school I had attended before coming to England. I explained that I had not attended any school since 1947 and had been working in a mechanical repair workshop for two years, before making the trip. He seemed somewhat taken aback by this and exclaimed, "Well, no wonder!"

Outside the classroom, I was beginning to find my feet. I was getting to grips with English money (pounds, shillings and pence) and discovering how many coupons were needed for an ounce of sweets. My new-found school companions showed me how to use the trolley buses and tube trains, took me shopping in 'Woolworse' (Woolworths) and showed me the swimming baths in Hornsea.

With the help of the social workers and some of the other friendly women at the workhouse, the rest of the family were also settling in. The financial situation must have also improved somewhat, because Mum was now able to give us small amounts of pocket money when we asked for it.

Halfway House

After staying about two months in the workhouse, we were moved to a Halfway House situated in a place called Plumstead, near Woolwich in South East London. This turned out to be very much like the workhouse, in that it was another Victorian building, divided into compartmented rooms. It had originally been part of the hospital next door but had been converted to accommodate displaced families, who were waiting to be allocated council housing after the war. There were many more families here than at the workhouse! Like the workhouse, men were not permitted to stay overnight and the women kept the place clean and worked in the kitchen, in return for food and shelter. Mum had to forfeit Father's pension to the Almoner, which left her very short of cash but at least we were a step closer to being housed in the London area.

Theo found a job as an assistant to a van driver delivering pies, while the rest of us were again registered in local schools. My school was Wycombe Lane Secondary Modern and I got a daily free ride to and from school on a trolley bus. The boys at this school were much the same as the previous one; however, I was told that, because it was close to the border with Kent, (where hops are grown and traditionally harvested by members of the gypsy community), the school had a sizeable number of gypsy kids. I had never seen or met a gypsy before and had no concept of what they looked or behaved like. I soon learnt though that they were a law unto themselves and I was warned by the other kids to keep well clear!

Although I managed to impress Mr Bourne, the games teacher, during PE lessons he was also my Form and English teacher and was much less impressed with my written English. One day, he asked me to stay behind while the others went for mid-afternoon break.

He questioned me about the poor quality of my work saying that he didn't understand why a seemingly intelligent boy of my age could be so far behind with written work, when my oral English was better than most pupils in the school. "You understand instructions quite clearly and seem confident in the gym and at games. What did your teachers think of you in your last school?" he asked. I explained that I had only attended my last school for about two months and there they had identified the same problem. I repeated the story of my absence from school since 1947 and the reasons why. He sat back in his chair wide-eyed and said, "I'm so sorry lad. Of course - that would explain everything."

The Maths teacher, who said he had once worked at a school in India, also questioned me about my poor performance. He said that he expected a much better standard of work from me as, in his opinion, education in Indian schools was of a much higher quality. I had to go through the process of explaining my school history to him as well. He then asked me if I was an Anglo-Indian. I replied, "I'm not sure sir, I was never told about that."

Mr Bourne was taking the class for Games in the gym one day. He got out some boxing gloves from a cupboard and raised one pair above his head, saying, "Who's going to be first?" My hand went up quickly. He threw one pair of gloves to me and put the other pair on himself, saying that we were going to learn the art of boxing. He told the rest of the boys to form a circle around us and, after roughly going through the rules and defining the target area, he squared up to me. He was quite a small, slightly-built man and he didn't look at all athletic; he spoke with what I thought was a superior English accent. He didn't even get changed to teach Games as a rule; he usually just took off his jacket and slipped into a pair of soft, black leather shoes. Oddly, he would keep his waistcoat on!

Thinking he meant us to spar, I saw a chance to land a couple of left jabs to his head. He walked straight into them and both got home, causing him to flinch. I wasn't sure if he had expected me to throw any punches but I was just about to drive home a straight right when he covered up his right eye with a glove. One of my left jabs had caught him in the eye and blurred his vision temporarily; I pulled back, apologising. He looked a little embarrassed and the rest of the class began to snigger. He said, "There's nothing funny about it - the glove lace caught me in the eye, that's all!" Later he called me aside and asked me where I had learnt to box. I told him that it was one of the main sports at the Army boarding school I had attended in India. "That's why you were the first to raise a hand when I asked," he said. His eye was still watering and red but he managed to crack a smile. I don't think he had ever had a pair of boxing gloves on in his life before, as he seemed too clumsy.

Joe and Matt Emmett

At the next break-time some kids approached me. One of them said, "Hey! I heard you KOd one of the teachers in the gym." I smiled and stupidly said that I hadn't - but if he'd have given me any lip I would have done; they laughed! These kids looked shabbily dressed with tangled, uncombed hair but they seemed friendly enough. One of them was called Joe; another said his name was Matt. I began to meet up with them during breaks and sometimes outside school as well. They were a bit wild and cheeky to other people but, somehow, being with them gave me a bit more confidence and I began to copy some of their behaviour. Mr Bourne noticed this and asked to speak to me one day.

He told me that, when I had arrived at the school, he had thought I would be a good influence on the rest of the boys. Now, it appeared that I had chosen to associate with the more troublesome ones. He warned me to stay away from them, or else I would end up in trouble. I wanted to heed his advice but I felt trapped. On the one hand, I knew that Mr Bourne was right; on the other, if I stopped associating with Joe and Matt I would be betraying their friendship and they might resent it. I didn't want to risk their displeasure; by the same token, I knew that if I needed support in the future, the Emmetts could be valuable allies, as the other kids were scared of them.

Joe and Matt were poorly dressed but they always seemed to have plenty of pocket money. I met up with them in Plumstead High Street one day, where they had invited me to accompany them doing their Christmas shopping. At first I had declined, as I had no money - at which they had both laughed and retorted, "You don't need money, when you go shopping in Woolworse." We duly headed for Woolworths where Joe produced a cloth shopping bag, which he had folded and stuffed up his jumper. He began to explain how they did their shopping: "Matt and me hold one handle each, to keep the bag open below the counter where the girls won't be able to see it. When we see something we like, we pick two of 'em up, hold 'em over the bag and pretend to look at 'em, while dropping one into the bag. Then we put the other one back on the counter. OK? Be careful to only pick up small things that you can hold with one hand."

I watched them as they made their way around. They made it look so simple that, even though I was watching them, I hardly noticed what they were getting up to. Then Joe said, "If you see something you like, come in the middle of us and do the same." I started to feel very nervous. I couldn't make up my mind whether or not to take anything but felt under pressure to do so. Eventually I saw some attractive, colourful marbles, packaged in net bags. On impulse, I picked up two bags and nervously dropped one into the bag. Unfortunately, this made a loud noise as it struck the other items in there, immediately alerting a counter assistant. She turned her head in our direction, saying, "What are you boys up to?" Then, leaning across the counter, she spotted the bag. Joe and Matt quickly began to make their way towards the door, weaving their way through customers and leaving me rooted to the spot. As they made their exit my eyes turned to a man in pursuit; I stayed put. The man pushed the door open and shouted after them but didn't give chase. Instead, he turned and asked the counter assistant if she would recognise them again. Pointing to me she replied, "He was with them."

The man came over to me and made me turn out my pockets. While I was doing so, he kept asking my name, the names of the others and which school I went to. Instinctively, I gave him my name and the name of the school but thought it best to deny knowing who the other boys were. The man shouted to the assistant, "Are you sure it was him? He's got nothing on him." After inspecting the floor where we had been standing, he asked where I lived and I told him. "We've had trouble with kids from there before," he said. Then he told me to leave the shop and not come back. I quietly made my way out and back to the Halfway House.

At the following Monday morning assembly, the Headmaster announced that everyone was to stay where they were until told to go back to class once assembly was over. A man and a woman walked into the hall with one of the teachers and we were instructed to be quiet and look to the front. I recognised them both as the staff that had apprehended me in Woolworths! I became very nervous as they approached but, for some reason; they passed me by without saying anything.

We returned to class and, when Mr Bourne had completed the attendance register, he told me to stand outside the classroom and wait for him there. When he came out he said, "You'd better come with me, Smith." I followed him to the Common Room. He opened the door and said, "In here, Smith." I stood by a table and he sat down. Speaking in his superior English accent he said, "I'm not too surprised that this has happened. Your name has been mentioned in connection with an incident in Woolworths on Saturday but, before we go any further, I want you to understand that, if you tell me the truth, I will try to help you. Now, tell me, were you involved?" I hung my head in shame and felt as if someone had fired a cannon ball into the pit of my stomach; the silence that followed spoke volumes. He said, "Look at me Smith. Now - were you involved?" I nodded but quickly added, "I didn't take anything, sir, but I was there." There was another short silence then the next question, "I don't suppose you'll want to tell me who was with you?" "No sir," I replied. "Well, I have a good idea who it was and you can't say that I didn't warn you. I don't know how far this is going to go but I believe that you are being led by the company you're keeping, so I'm going to stick my neck out for you. I'll see what I can do." He told me to go back to the class and I slunk back sheepishly. Again, I was being pulled in two directions; of course he was right but trying to avoid Joe and Matt in the school grounds was going to be really difficult. I decided to stay away from school for a few days in the hope that when I went back everything would have blown over.

He's Been Found!

It was just as well that I did! One day, during my self-imposed exile, Mum was summoned to the Warden's office at the Halfway House to be told that Father had been found and was now a patient at the Princess Beatrice Hospital in Earl's Court. She was quite upset to discover that the hospital was near to the SSAFA house, where we had first been taken, just months before. After being given directions by the Warden, Mum and I set about finding our way across London by train and bus. We had to change buses near Trafalgar Square; I remember walking across the square and a man persuading us to have our photograph taken with the pigeons, then charging us 1s 6d for it - that was Mum's cigarette money! When we eventually managed to get to the hospital it was outside visiting hours but, after we explained the circumstances, they gave Mum special permission to see Father.

I was not allowed to accompany her, as under-sixteens were not generally permitted entry to hospital in England at the time - not as visitors. It transpired that, at some point, Father must have collapsed somewhere - whether from his TB, from emotional strain, or a combination of the two is not clear - and the information he had given to the ambulance personnel had become mixed up with someone else's details. I can only think that he must have been disorientated and would have had great difficulty explaining the intricacies of our situation, even if anyone had been able to grasp them. The hospital authorities had no idea where we were and we didn't know where he was. Father thought that Mum had abandoned him; meanwhile, Mum and the SSAFA people - having been unable to find any information about him - decided that Father had abandoned the family! When I think about it now, I still find it very difficult to believe that we had originally been living no more than ten minutes' walk away from the hospital in Earl's Court but it still took the authorities over four months to trace our whereabouts. The doctors at the hospital told Mum that Father had been very ill and that, when his condition had improved enough to withstand major surgery, they would have to remove his entire left lung and a portion of the right lung as well. Mum began to visit Father regularly on Sunday and Wednesday afternoons. This meant that either Theo or I would have to accompany her for the journey, and then kill half an hour by walking around Earl's Court. It also meant extra expense, which we could ill afford; Mum liked a smoke and finding the money for bus fares and cigarettes was almost impossible. Even so, now and again she managed to save just enough to get five Woodbines from a nearby newsagent.

After Theo joined the Merchant Navy, it fell to me to accompany Mum on visiting days. I was always more than willing to do so, as it meant that I had to take Wednesday afternoons off school. I couldn't settle down to any school work anyway; it was not only the same old problem with reading and writing but also the legacy of going out to work for two years, back in Quetta. I resented having to go back to school all over again. Hence, my attendance became erratic, causing the School Attendance Monitor to pay Mum regular visits.

The cold and gloom of my first English winter - the winter of 1952 - began to bite deep; it affected the whole family. We experienced the horror of 'smog', which hung around for days, sometimes becoming so bad that it slowed the transport system to a crawl. The bus ticket collectors would have to walk in front of the buses with flame torches to guide the driver, even during the daytime. I remember going to the pictures and having to watch a film through a thick brown haze, which the powerful beam of light from the projector struggled to cut through. Strangely, I can't remember having an overcoat to wear through all this terrible weather. Christmas came and went without much ceremony; there was no money for toys or presents, just some clothes donated by the Red Cross and, of course, Christmas dinner, courtesy of the Halfway House.

I was now becoming quite familiar with the transport system. My confidence had increased and I could find my way into central London and back unaided. I developed a much better understanding of the currency and became accustomed to the cockney accent and all its slang. It was probably about this time that I developed some personal aspirations and, as I was now almost fifteen years old, I couldn't wait to leave school to start work.

A couple of kids at school had been given a pair of Lee Cooper blue jeans for Christmas and one of them was in my class. He wore the jeans to school one day, which of course attracted the attention of the rest of the boys, who drooled over them. Mr Bourne told him that they were working overalls and he should not wear them to school again. This jogged my memory of an Afghan lad at my workplace in Quetta, who wore a similar pair of trousers to work one day; he had said that he bought them from a market vendor, who imported used clothing from America. The colour and shape of the jeans and the copper rivets on the rear pockets had looked quite distinctive and I had been quite taken with them, but I had forgotten about them until now; I set my mind on getting myself a pair.

I suppose in today's jargon, you would say that they were on my 'urgent wish-list'. I reckon the price of a pair of Lee Cooper jeans in 1952/3 would have been about four or five shillings, but I knew there was no hope of me ever getting that kind of money. I applied at the local newsagent for a paper round but was told there were no vacancies at that time and I would have to wait.

It was at the newsagent's one day, when I was buying Mum's Woodbines, that I bumped into Joe and Matt. We exchanged pleasantries and the conversation turned to my quest to own a pair of jeans. Joe said we could easily get five shillings each by selling old lead - at which my ears pricked up. "How?" I asked. "I know where we could get a load of lead easily and my uncle can sell it for us," answered Joe; I was intrigued. "Come on I'll show you," he said. "Wait 'til I take these fags back to my Mum and I'll be back," I replied...

Gripped by a sense of urgency, I completed my errand and hurried back to find them waiting on the corner. As usual, Joe led the way; Matt was always the more passive of the two. It was early February and must have been after four o'clock in the afternoon, as it was dark. There was a lane with low, stone walls on either side. I could see a church on one side of the road and a large building on the other; Joe led us towards the latter. He pointed to a part of the building with a flat roof, saying, "Matt and me can get on that roof and chuck the lead down. You pick it up and throw it over the wall into the lane. Afterwards, we'll put it into a heap, stamp it flat and cover it up with grass and nettles. My uncle will come later and pick it up with his cart, OK?" In a mixed state of fear and excitement I nodded agreement, without really grasping what I was letting myself in for. Joe added, "Keep looking down the lane and tell us if anyone is coming."

I really had no idea of what they meant by 'lead'; the only lead I had ever seen were the tiny weights in Papa's fishing-tackle box but I didn't want to show my ignorance. Joe and Matt shinned up a drainpipe; then, after a while, they started throwing strips of stuff off the roof. It was coming down fast. I took one look and began to pick up the strips and run to the wall, but the first load was too heavy and I didn't quite make it over the wall. Each time I picked up a piece my fingers became colder and colder. The operation hadn't got far, when I heard a man's voice coming from the direction of the churchyard, on the other side of the lane. "What are you boys doing?" I looked up to see that both Joe and Matt had disappeared, so I hastily made a run for the gate. The man beat me to it and, while I was trying to deal with the latch, he grabbed me by the wrist saying, "Don't worry, I won't hurt you - just tell me what you were doing in there." In a voice filled with fear I said that I was lost and was trying to find my way home.

The man spoke with a cultured accent. He tried to calm me down and, releasing his grip on my wrists said, "Where is your home, son?" Having made a confused attempt to lie my way out of the situation, I began to search for the words and 'Rest Centre' came out. "I know where it is," he said, "But you must explain what you and the other boys were up to." "We were just mucking about sir," I said. "All right, just tell me your name and what school you attend; then I'll show you how to get back to the Rest Centre." Relieved that he was going to let me go, I told him my name and that I went to Wycombe Lane Secondary School. "Very well but if I find out that you've been up to no good I will be seeing your Headmaster." Although this sounded ominous, the threat of unpleasantness to come was drowned by the instant relief of escape.

I stayed away from school for another couple of days. When I did decide to go back Mr Bourne told me to wait outside the classroom after morning register. When he appeared he said, "Come on Smith," and promptly escorted me to the office of the Headmaster, Mr Wade. Mr Wade began by saying, "Smith, very shortly you will be leaving school. Your short stay with us has not given Mr Bourne or me time to make a proper assessment of your potential. However, from what Mr Bourne tells me, it would seem that you are in a hurry to leave school and begin work. I have no idea how you intend to earn a living, because your attendance record is appalling and your school work is some of the worst I have ever seen. Mr Bourne tells me that your moral behaviour has steadily declined, due to your persistence in keeping company with troublesome elements outside school hours. Within the last couple of days I've received a complaint that you were involved in an incident at a building belonging to the church. You can thank your lucky stars that the church authorities have been very lenient by not taking the matter any further. However, I am writing to your parents, requesting a meeting with them. I shall be discussing with them the possibility of you attending a corrective training establishment, in order to prepare you for suitable employment. Do you have any idea what you would like to do?" I was caught completely off guard and couldn't think of anything to say. "Well?" he urged me. Theo had only recently joined the Merchant Navy so, without much further thought I said, "The Merchant Navy, sir." "Very well," said Mr Wade.

Bad Boy

Mum was summoned to the school and advised of a plan to have me admitted to the Indefatigable and National Sea Training School for Boys, in Anglesey, North Wales. There I would receive training to prepare me for a career in either the Royal Navy or the Merchant Navy. So, in late April 1953, at the age of fifteen, I was given a travel warrant and directions to make my own way to the Sailors' Home in Liverpool. I was told that I would be met by an agent, who would organise my transfer to the training establishment at Plas Llanfair, Anglesey. I had no idea where Liverpool was and even less idea about Wales. With my small, battered suitcase, containing a change of underwear and some toiletries, I embarked upon my first long train journey in England. I managed to find my way from Plumstead to Euston Station but not without stopping frequently to ask directions!

I boarded a steam train at Euston and, as soon as we pulled away from the city, my attention was fixed on the countryside. It was mesmerising! The towns, villages and farming communities all seemed so completely different and ultra-civilised compared to those I had been accustomed to seeing when travelling on trains through India. After changing trains at Crewe, I finally arrived at Liverpool's Lime Street Station and made my way to the ticket barrier. I was about to ask the ticket collector for directions to the Sailors' Home when a man in a trilby hat and scruffy raincoat tapped me on the head and asked if my name was Ian Smith - to which I answered, "Yes sir." "Come with me, boy," he said and led me out of the station, where we jumped on a bus which took us to the Sailors' Home. He booked me in and handed me the key to my room, saying that I would have to stay there for a couple of days and wait for the arrival of some other boys; then we would all be travelling together to the training school in Wales.

The Sailors' Home, I discovered, was a four-storey Victorian prison building. Its cells had been converted into basic rooms, containing just an iron bedstead, a small table and a chair. Evidently, little had changed since the place was a working prison; all the rooms led out onto balconied landings and heavy wire mesh covered the central part of each landing, to prevent suicidal inmates from jumping to their deaths, or being thrown over the balcony by an irate fellow-prisoner, presumably!

A couple of days later the man in the trilby hat and scruffy raincoat returned. By then, there were about eight or ten other boys, including myself, and he put us all on a train for the Isle of Anglesey. Eventually, we arrived at a village with the longest place name in Europe and the second longest official one-word place name in the world - the sign at the station was very impressive! I later learnt that, for short, it was called Plas Llanfair PG, which was far easier to remember! A man dressed in a naval officer's uniform greeted us and organised us into two parallel lines. He then marched us for about a mile and a half down an unsurfaced road, to the Indefatigable and National Sea Training School for Boys, where I would have to spend the next year of my life. It was situated on the banks of the Menai Straits, which flow between the Isle of Anglesey and mainland Wales. From selected vantage points, Mount Snowdon - which I had never heard of before - could be seen.

During the train journey, the conversation among the boys had suggested that the school was going to be a tough place to survive in. The officer who marched us down resembled and behaved like an over-sized bad-tempered bulldog, a fact which did nothing to ease our fears. Later, we learnt that he was an ex Royal Navy Physical Training Instructor, named Mr Mugridge and he was known to be a bit of a tyrant!

Despite all of this, within a couple of weeks I discovered that the place was full of kids who were guilty of committing nothing more serious than a couple of minor misdemeanours; in fact, they were pretty much a bunch of pussy-cats! There were two hundred trainees, organised into four divisions: Rodney, Raleigh, Hood and Drake - I was in Drake. Full naval rating uniform was worn for best, with shorts and long socks for everyday wear. Each division contained fifty boys, most of whom had never been away from home before and suffered chronic homesickness.

The staff soon spotted that I was no stranger to military-type foot drill and the discipline that accompanied it. Hence, in a short space of time, I was promoted to Leading Hand, a role which carried with it certain responsibilities but also some privileges. The Chief Officer was so impressed with my attention to tidiness and my knowledge of drill that, to my embarrassment, he would sometimes call on me to demonstrate to newcomers who were having problems with coordination. The same officer was also instrumental in having me selected, along with five other boys, to attend the coronation of Queen Elizabeth II on 2nd June 1953.

We travelled to London on the day before the coronation and stayed at the Union Jack Club overnight. The next morning, at about 5.30am, the Chief Officer and the six of us assembled, with a huge contingent of Navy, Army and Air Force personnel, on Horse Guards Parade. The Chief Officer took the opportunity to remind us that we were highly privileged to witness such an historic occasion and that it was something we would remember for the rest of our lives. Along with the rest of the contingent, we were then marched down the Mall to take up our positions on the Victoria Memorial, in front of Buckingham Palace, where we were to spend the entire day. In the pouring rain, with only two opportunities all day to cross the road into Hyde Park to relieve ourselves and with a packed lunch of a couple of sandwiches, an orange and nothing to drink, the whole thing felt more like a punishment than a privilege.

Away to Sea

In January 1954, I was called into the office and informed that I had earned three months' remission and, as such, was to be prepared for discharge. The options on offer were: enlist in the Royal Navy (which the school highly recommended), or one of the other Armed Forces - all of which involved passing a written test. Alternatively, join The Merchant Navy (no written test), or be free to return home. I decided on the Merchant Navy and joined in March 1954.

I caught a train to Liverpool and booked into the Sailors' Home for a couple of days, before meeting up with the agent in the trilby hat and scruffy raincoat; he helped me with the registration process. A few days later, I was informed that he had found a very good ship for me and so it was that I caught the overhead railway to Brunswick Dock and signed on to the Kumasi Palm.

Ian Smith, age 15, Merchant Navy

On the day we were to leave Liverpool for the west coast of Africa, there was the 'first tripper's' initiation ceremony to contend with; this consisted of me being dragged to the nearest alehouse and having beer practically poured down my throat! After downing two pints of brown and mild - my first ever taste of alcohol - I lost my sense of direction and coordination of my limbs! I don't recall boarding the ship but was informed later that the Bosun had to have me removed from deck and placed in my cabin, where I was allowed to sleep it off. Some time later I was woken by a rumbling noise and an urgent need to regurgitate the two pints of ale I had been obliged to force down earlier. I managed to make it to the ship's rails in time to donate the contents of my stomach to the River Mersey. The rumbling noise that woke me was the ship's propeller churning up the murky river water. A mug of black coffee was thrust in my direction with the words, "Hey'ar, lad, get this down your neck." It was the guy I was to share a cabin with, Albert Ungi; he was half-Filipino, half-Rottweiler - a seasoned sea dog who hailed from the Dingle end of Liverpool.

Albert advised, "You berrer get yer 'ed down till the mornin' lad." I didn't argue. The next day, I met the Bosun and he explained the duties I was expected to undertake as the 'Peggy' or Mess Steward. I was to take care of the needs of twelve members of the deck crew, nine of whom would be around-the-clock watchkeepers and three would be on day work. The watchkeepers were split into three groups of three men for each four hour watch, 8pm to midnight, midnight to 4am and 4am to 8am. They would take their turns at the ship's wheel and keep lookout during the night; in the daytime no lookout was necessary, apart from in exceptional weather conditions. The day workers, and those not on watch, were involved in the routine maintenance of the vessel's superstructure, owing to the corrosive effects of salt water. Other deck duties included maintenance of all the running gear, such as ropes, steel cables and hawsers. There were other members of the deck crew whose accommodation was separate from ours (the Bosun, Lamp Trimmer and Carpenter), but they all took care of themselves.

I had to fetch hot meals for the deck crew from the galley three times a day, wash all the dishes and cutlery, scrub the floor and tabletops of the mess-deck and pantry every night, draw and monitor a continuous stock of dry stores and maintain a high level of cleanliness. I was also to provide mugs of tea for the deck crew at break times twice a day, during which they would take full advantage of my raw naivety and make me the butt of their insults and childish jokes. Albert said, "You don't have to take that crap lad - just give them as good as you get. Don't worry; I won't let any of them harm you." But Albert never seemed to be around when he was needed!

For the first three days of the trip, I felt that I was either still suffering the lingering effects of the two pints of ale, or else experiencing my premature demise; I prayed for the ship to be still long enough for me to make it to the toilet and rid myself of my stomach contents. The cook kindly offered me a cure, handing me a piece of fatty bacon on a length of string, saying, "Just slide it up and down your throat lad, that'll cure yer, ha, ha, ha!"; needless to say, this was yet another of the well-worn pranks of my shipmates! I had an urgent feeling that if I managed to survive, I would jump off this ship at the first glimpse of land. I complained to Albert, "Nobody cares how bad I'm feeling!" He laughed out loud, "If you expect any sympathy lad, you should never have left your mummy's side!" He added that, in this game, I would have to learn to deal with people of dubious character, low morals and no regard for others. The dregs of life, in other words - and the sooner I got used to it, the better!

About four or five days into the voyage, we arrived at Las Palmas to take on fuel. This should have taken only a few hours but it was there that I witnessed, for the first time, scenes of extreme drunkenness. Some members of the crew, who had gone ashore at lunchtime, were so intoxicated that they had to be rounded up by the Bosun and a junior officer and escorted back to the ship. The ship's departure had to be delayed by almost an hour, costing the company extra harbour fees. I was placed on cast-off duty on the forecastle, as a result of the acute lack of sober deck hands! This was not something that would normally be expected of an inexperienced first trip deck boy. In fact, I was told later that it may have contravened Board of Trade safety regulations.

While waiting on standby for the drunken crew members to be rounded up, I witnessed an event that will stay with me for the rest my life. I watched a drunken man struggling to walk in a straight line, while making his way down the quay towards the ship. He suddenly veered to his right and fell off the dockside into the water. Some dock workers threw him a lifebelt but he made no effort to grab it and he sank rapidly. We later discovered that the man had been one of our crew members and, to make matters worse, we heard that he had left a wife and three small children. The Kumasi Palm departed Las Palmas, minus a laundry man.

The living conditions for the deck crew and firemen were cramped and basic, the cabins being referred to by the men as 'pig pens'. When I finally began to get into the routine of things, I was persuaded by some crew members to clean their cabins, wash underwear and shirts and roll cigarettes for those going on watch. These favours, though voluntary, were carried out with the expectation of a whip-round at the end of the voyage - a long-standing tradition, I was told. Later in the voyage, upon entering port, I decided to indulge in a little private enterprise and offered an ironing service to the other sailors; my rates were 6d for a shirt and a shilling for trousers. The proceeds enabled me to buy my first pair of blue jeans, at long last! Ironing was a little trick that I had picked up while watching my *ayah* at work with a heavy charcoal iron when I was a boy in India.

Liverpudlians are renowned for their sharp wit and sense of humour. Initially, there was a period of geniality among the crew, but I sensed that it was tinged with a degree of caution; I was told that some of the men aboard ship were from notorious areas of Liverpool and I found that people from those disadvantaged areas had a strong sense of self-preservation. I learnt that Albert Ungi, my cabin mate, was a member of a Filipino gang; Tom Melia was a member of a gang called 'The Brothers', while Tony Smith was a member of the most feared gang at that time: 'The Peanut Gang'. This toxic mixture of dubious individuals created an uneasy atmosphere, not only for me but also for the other, less criminally-inclined members of the crew.

As the trip wore on, the mood among some of the crew gradually changed, eventually becoming openly hostile. Although I tried to avoid getting involved in their exchanges, the men used me as a go-between to deliver insults and threats to each other. All conversations seemed to be dominated by football, beer and women, which caused many arguments and disputes. I found it very difficult to understand the extreme fanatical worship of football clubs and tried to remain impartial, declaring no preference for either Everton or Liverpool; because of this, I was deemed the lowest life on the ship. I was told that, if the ship were to go down, I would be the last to leave. That is, after the ship's cat had been taken off safely!

Disillusioned

As the voyage progressed I began to realise that being a sailor was not the idyllic life I had imagined it would be. Perhaps all the recent upheaval in my life was now catching up with me and was beginning to affect my outlook on life; the future no longer seemed so rosy. At sixteen I was not mature enough to rationalise my situation but I was beginning to feel that forces outside my control were dictating the course of my life. Looking back I can see that, although I was enjoying the freedom to express my suppressed childhood emotions, I couldn't reconcile this with my strict regimental upbringing. At times I enjoyed the liberating atmosphere but, at others, I felt oppressed by the hostile behaviour of some of the men I was living amongst; in their eyes, I was the lowest form of life on board and, as such, a legitimate target for their bullying, boorish behaviour.

A mere two years earlier, I had left behind a virtual Third World existence, with the expectation that I would integrate into the 'mother culture'. Now my understanding of that culture was being confounded by the behaviour of some its more questionable elements. My life had altered too dramatically and too fast and I was not equipped to deal with such a testing disappointment. With no opportunity to seek counsel from sympathetic adults, I felt weak and confused.

Our voyage continued south, along the coast of West Africa. After calling at the larger ports, like Monrovia, Free Town, Accra and Lagos we began to make our way to some of the more obscure 'creeks' (narrow inlets), such as Ports Harcourt and Calabar. Here, access for ships larger than 25,000 tons was so narrow, they could only leave by going astern (i.e. in reverse). The mosquito- and mango fly-infested conditions, plus the searing, inescapable heat, made it difficult to maintain a cheerful outlook on life. I was continually told by the others that this area was known as the 'White Man's Grave' and I began to understand why the men drank themselves into oblivion at every given opportunity.

Day by day, without realising it, I was becoming assimilated into the crude culture of sea-going men; over the next three months, my behaviour began to mirror that of my compulsory companions. The need to be accepted became paramount and it was becoming clear that I would have to develop a hard front, in order to survive in the Merchant Navy - as Albert Ungi frequently reminded me. With his words constantly ringing in my ears, I adopted the false persona of the 'hard man'; it was my futile and mistaken belief that this was the only way to deal with threats. I began to smoke, to use foul language routinely and to take part in mindless drunken antics and, at times, ending up in a state of complete oblivion. Little did I realise how stupid it must have looked to others. The trip lasted three months and, on our return to Liverpool, I signed off, vowing never ever to sail with the Palm Line again!

A Second Chance

With no alternative employment prospects I reluctantly made a decision to remain in the Merchant Navy. However, I resolved to seek out shipping companies with a better reputation for crew accommodation – companies who would never employ the kind of lowlife I had the misfortune to sail with on the Kumasi Palm!

After a week's visit to the family - who, by now, were well settled into a council flat in North London - I returned to Liverpool and booked into the Sailors' Home. It was 'cheap' but failed the test of 'cheerful'! While waiting to find a suitable ship to sign on to, I sought the advice of an old hand over a game of snooker; he gave me what seemed like good information and named some of the shipping companies to avoid. He also agreed to accompany me to the shipping pool the next morning to see what was available and advise accordingly.

The following day, as we approached the shipping clerk's counter, I noted the heavy metal grille through which we had to speak. My experienced new mate proceeded to explain my situation. The clerk looked through a ledger, saying that he could offer me the choice of two small coastal vessels or one deep-sea vessel called the John Holt, which sailed between Liverpool and the west coast of Africa. The old hand advised me that coastal vessels were only licensed to sail in home or continental waters and were usually crewed by family men, or those who just preferred shorter periods away from home. The downside was that they also accepted seamen with dubious conduct records, who had been blacklisted by deep-sea shipping companies; I didn't fancy that! My heart sank when the clerk said that I would have to sign articles that very afternoon if I accepted the offer.

The old guy said to me, "It looks like you're left with only one option," but added that, although he had never sailed with the Holt Shipping Company, neither had he heard any bad reports about them. Having parted with some of my earnings at home, and with funds running short, I agreed, with some trepidation, to have a look at the John Holt. I took the overhead railway to Brunswick Dock where she was berthed and I spoke to the Bosun, who explained that the Holt Shipping Company was a family-run business and that their ships carried general cargo from Liverpool to West Africa, returning with a main cargo of copper ingots from ports along the River Congo. This would involve a round trip of around three months. The ship was a clean-looking freighter of 2,159 tons, less than half the size of the Kumasi Palm and the crew's accommodation looked so much better. Therefore, despite my misgivings, I agreed to sign on.

On meeting the rest of the crew my first impression was that they seemed an improvement on the last lot; they even looked less threatening. When I mentioned the names of the men I had sailed with previously, they sympathised, "You poor little sod!" However, I was still not too sure of a couple of them, so I kept up my guard and my defensive attitude. My cabin mate, Alan Hutchinson, was a rather small but amenable chap, who had been with the company for two years and in the Merchant Navy since leaving school. This was reassurance enough for me to relax a little bit. Alan was a keen photographer, who developed his own negatives and prints; later during the trip he got me interested in photography and took time to teach me the basics. He was a great help to me generally, as there wasn't much he didn't know about seamanship and I was so grateful to have him as a cabin mate. As the voyage progressed my fears melted away and I was able to relax.

After discharging most of our cargo at ports along the West African coast, we made our way to the mouth of the River Congo. Our first port of call was Boma and the next stop would be Leopoldville. The news came through that heavy rains up country had caused extensive flooding inland. Alan said that navigating further up the fast-running river was going to present big problems, particularly through a notorious section called 'Hell's Gates', where giant whirlpools and eddies would cause the handling of ships to become very difficult. Now that most of the cargo had been offloaded, the ship was sitting high in the water and Alan advised that the rudder would therefore become less efficient. As we began heading further up the Congo all hands were put on standby and engine room staff rehearsed their emergency drill; helmsmen would need to be relieved every half hour, instead of the usual two hours. Alan said that he had never seen the river running so fast before and there was an air of concern among the older sea dogs. At times the ship banked violently from port to starboard and back again and was frequently diverted off course by the force of the current. After a day of slow progress through these unpredictable currents, we finally reached the port of Leopoldville.

While we were in port, unloading the last of our cargo, I noticed something familiar in the way the native population were being treated. It felt similar to the conditions of colonial rule in India, only here the regime was far more overt. Alan told me that the indigenous population were highly regulated; for example it was compulsory for all Africans to carry an identity card. They also lived in officially-designated compounds and were subject to a night-time curfew. Only those with special permission, who were employed in the service of the white population, were allowed out of their compounds - the fenced-off encampments where they were obliged to live. During curfew hours they had to wear a white cotton jacket to signify that privilege.

I noticed that some undernourished young kids, both girls and boys, were being allowed on board and curiously, that they each carried a pair of old tailoring scissors. They spoke no English but, instead, would look you in the eye and work the scissors a couple of times. I asked Alan what these kids were doing and he explained that in the Belgian Congo begging carried a prison sentence, so they carried a pair of scissors to indicate that they were earning rewards by carrying out minor clothing repairs. The kids seemed to hang around the galley and the seaman's mess at meal times, so I got the message and made a point of saving any leftovers for them. On one occasion there seemed to be rather a lot of food left over from dinner so, when the kids appeared, I handed it to them with a big grin on my face. I felt pleased with myself and quite benevolent, only to discover later that one of the crew had not yet had his dinner! When I turned in that night, my mind wandered back to times in Quetta and our destitute neighbours, the Hannah family, and I became quite emotional.

While clearing the tables after lunch one day I heard an awful commotion on the dockside; I poked my head out of the porthole and saw a man writhing in agony with his foot jammed between the twin tyres of a truck. Somehow, the truck had reversed suddenly, knocking him over and running over his foot; he was obviously suffering agonising pain and was screaming, while his fellow workers tried to release his leg from under the truck. A policeman arrived on the scene and began to shove and push the crowd away, then kept gesturing to the poor man to stop making a fuss. Nevertheless, the man continued to scream and shout in agony, to the point where the policeman became so annoyed he began to display his temper by shouting threats and showing his bull-whip; however the man still refused to stop screaming. Suddenly, the policeman uncoiled his whip and unleashed several blows around the man's face and upper body. By now the commotion had attracted the attention of some of the officers and crew on board and they began to shout at the policeman to stop. Eventually one of the officers was sent onto the dock to further persuade the policeman to back off. I remember being quite horrified at such a brutal spectacle.

As a Deck Boy, my duties were just as they had been on the Kumasi Palm but on this ship, I was encouraged by the Bosun to take part in other duties, in order to gain more practical seamanship. Alan, my cabin mate saw to it that I put in the required ten hours of experience at the ship's helm, to progress to the next stage of proficiency: Junior Ordinary Seaman.

On my return to Liverpool, in September 1954, I signed off from the John Holt, with a revised opinion of what the Merchant Navy promised for the future. During the following years, the Merchant Navy gave me the opportunity to visit some of the most celebrated capitals of the world, as well as many lesser-known ones. I was privileged to enjoy many years of world travel and adventures, witnessing on my way both the magnificence and harshness of some of the most diverse societies on this planet.

Epilogue

Eventually I found myself becoming more at ease with sea-going life and my initial anxieties were eased. My new career was giving me the opportunity to rethink my previous understanding of character and social interactions; friendships were formed with some unlikely individuals and life was now taking on a very different colour. I felt more relaxed and I even indulged in socialising with my newly-formed friends. They introduced me to the delights of visiting pubs, music clubs and themed coffee houses, in and around the west end of London's Soho district. Here various stars of the future could be seen in the process of carving a future in entertainment - clubs such as Two Eyes, Freight Train, Flamingo, Ronnie Scott's and many too numerous to mention, where you would rub shoulders with the stars of the future. I also visited the various big name dance halls of the period, where famous disc jockeys played the then popular rock and roll records during lunch breaks and where you could jive your socks off for the ticket price of just 6 pence!

Inevitably a combination of naivety and poor judgement led me to stumble into rather more questionable establishments from time to time, especially during shore leave abroad. These places were often frequented by decidedly dodgy characters with alternative agendas! After several close shaves and an episode of overstaying my leave I received my National Service call-up papers. They arrived in January 1958, just in time, I now believe, to save me from drifting into more serious trouble.

In February of the same year I celebrated my twenty-first birthday and was assigned to guard duty with the Royal Army Ordinance Corps at Hilsea, near Portsmouth. On completion of basic training I was posted to 14 Battalion, based in Didcot in Berkshire. During my service there I met Isabel, a stunning-looking local girl, born and raised in the nearby village of East Hendred. We were married in the spring of 1962 and in the following years we raised four children: Nicholas, Teresa, Geoffrey and Darryl. I am proud to say that, judging by today's standards, their behaviour was positively angelic, never requiring more than minor chastisement! They have long since grown up and fled the nest but remain in regular contact. We also now have three lovely granddaughters: Christina, Jasmine and Adele. Needless to say both Isabel and I are very proud of them all.

As an uneducated individual, lacking any marketable skills, I depended on local employment opportunities to provide for my family. Fortunately, my ability to turn my hand to most practical situations (as a result, I believe, of the experiences I had as a child) meant that, during the course of my working life, I was able to find jobs in the construction industry, road haulage and motor vehicle assembly; then later on in newspaper production and professional photography. None of these occupations required academic ability as such, though my skill set grew increasingly technical over the years

Mechanical assembly work came easily to me, given my early hands-on experience, whereas my introduction to the printing industry came as a result of my self-taught interest in photography. In the 1970s I became deeply interested in the subject, probably in an attempt to relieve the mind-bending boredom of assembly line work. I borrowed some cash to make a down payment on my first 35mm camera but soon realised that it was going to be an expensive hobby; in order to make it self-funding I built a darkroom and set about producing photographs of local news events and submitting them to local newspapers on a freelance basis. Once I had become an established contributor the income from my photos allowed me to finance top quality equipment. I was able to produce acceptable professional photographs and the quality and content of them eventually caught the eye of the editorial staff. My confidence had grown with every assignment; finally I could rely on another source of income as an established freelance photographer, covering all aspects of the craft - including press, social and wedding photography.

In 1980 the MG car plant in Abingdon ceased production and closed. After fifteen years of service, along with the rest of the workforce, I was made redundant. A pretty bleak period followed: unemployment, interspersed with the kind of manual labour that finally did for my already damaged back. In 1983, I underwent major spinal surgery and a couple of lower discs were removed. Unfortunately this did not achieve the desired result and there followed a four and a half year period of painful recovery in which I was unable to do any useful work. In-between bouts of acute pain and disability I continued to keep up with my photography, while I constantly worried and wracked my brains as to whether or how I was going to earn a living in future. It was abundantly clear that any type of manual work would be out of the question.

It was during a visit to the offices of the local newspaper, (I was chaperoning one of my younger sons, who was doing some research for a school project at the time), that I got chatting with the head of the IT department. During the conversation, I casually mentioned that I was desperate to get back to full-time work. It so happened that he had a vacancy available in his department and, to my disbelief, he offered me a trial period. I didn't even let him finish his sentence; I snatched at the chance, even though the loss of sickness benefit would mean a considerable reduction in my income and my doctor needed some persuading to sign a back-to-work certificate - he had only recently stated I was to refrain from work for the next twelve months.

In the spring of 1988, and trembling with excitement, I reported for work at the offices of The Oxford and County Newspapers. My jaw dropped when it became clear that the job would involve dealing with the very thing that I had spent my life avoiding, i.e. reading! My principal task was to identify digitally printed copy (newspaper jargon for written content) and deliver it to the various publications in the Paste-up Department. After a couple of months of having to deal with my numerous errors, the supervisor of the department took me aside and asked if I had difficulty with the written word; I nodded apprehensively. To my surprise, he said, "Don't worry! I have a son with the same problem. I'll get you some help." Then the paste-up artists were instructed to come over to my desk and sort out their own bromide copy, rather than waiting for it. This would give me more time to concentrate and to make fewer mistakes and it seemed to work reasonably well.

After about six months, the manager of the Reprographics Department, which dealt with the processing of light sensitive material and the preparation of photographs for printing, approached me saying he was planning to fill a vacancy in his department. He told me that, as a photographer, I was just the sort of person he was looking for and then asked if I would be interested; "How soon can I start?" I replied. The new job would be ideal for me. It meant that I would be working in an environment within my comfort zone, my salary would double and I would be free to continue with my freelance work. I celebrated with a pint of bitter at a local pub called The Waterman's Arms, during my lunch break!

A speedy transfer was arranged and soon I was working in what they called the Process Department. Some union members of staff in the department were less than welcoming; occasionally they were openly hostile, questioning the validity of my appointment and complaining that they had been required to serve three-year apprenticeships to reach their skill level. I chose to ignore their remarks and persevered with my efforts to study computer technology and allied software. This I did by reading manuals during my lunch breaks and using available computer terminals during quiet periods at work. The fight-back took longer for me, owing to my difficulty with reading. However, after about nine months senior management summoned me to their office. They told me that my rapid progress had not gone unnoticed and that they proposed to send me on a two week course to further my knowledge with their colour picture-editing software. They said that my knowledge of photography and colour theory made me the ideal candidate for the course. They also told me that they were keen to increase the number of colour pages in their daily and weekly publications and they would need an extra member of staff to achieve this.

On my return from the course I was awarded full-skilled status and I could now face the cynics in the department on equal terms. Needless to say, I wasted no time in pressing home my own brand of cynicism, telling them, "If it took you people three years to attain skilled status, does it not strike you as odd that I managed to do the same in less than a year?" With my salary now doubled again, and with further income from photography, the family were at last able to enjoy some minor luxuries and it is fair to say that our standard of living from then on was higher than we had been used to, even before those grim years of recession, redundancy and unemployment in the early 1980s.

In all, I worked another fifteen years for Oxford and County Newspapers, before retiring in February 2003. Like any job it had its ups and downs and I was more than ready to hang up my work tie at the end. Being naturally combative I had borne some of the negatives with bad grace and had found myself in conflict with managers, colleagues - and sometimes even the hours and conditions, which had been subject to change and decline over the years. However, on balance, as well as some unaccustomed affluence, the job had given me things I couldn't put a price on: the opportunity to use and expand the technical knowledge which I had already absorbed, the chance to earn a living doing something that interested me and, at long last, it provided me with something that I knew I was really good at. This recognition of my competence and ability and the realisation that I was very far from being stupid, contrary to the message that had been hammered home during those dark days at school, meant more to me than anything.

I now live in retirement with my wife Isabel in a delightful rural setting in Oxfordshire, where we have lived for the past fifty-four years. I have continued to keep busy with my many and varied interests: photography (of course), family history (naturally), music, gardening, computer technology and all kinds of DIY projects – to name but a few. I am so grateful to have metamorphosed from a school boy who couldn't learn, into an adult who would not stop learning! Writing this memoir has been part of that learning process and I hope that my quest for knowledge will never cease!

"Hope springs eternal."
(Alexander Pope - "An Essay on Man.")

How this Book was Born

Looking back on the first sixteen years of my life, from the day of my birth in February 1938, to September 1954, I suspect that I may have encountered more eventful situations, during that short space of time, than many of my contemporaries. Life for my family was anything but easy, in a land-locked region of the subcontinent of India. I witnessed the last vestiges of British rule in India and, with it, the upheaval and carnage of independence from Britain. This was the time when the indigenous population began to exact retribution on their former rulers, forcing their tormentors to abandon the country and flee.

Through the medium of my story I hope that I may have opened a window on what life was like for many other Anglo-Indian boys like me, growing up through this troubled and challenging period of British history. As a functional illiterate and an unqualified individual, whose early course of life was dictated by so many conflicting demands, I hope that I may now be permitted to indulge myself with a modicum of dignity.

Further Information

Unlike some families, ours cannot not be described as 'close-knit'. Quite soon after arriving in England events began to place us in various parts of the country. Apart from my parents and my younger sister Deanna and young brother Ken, we're all still alive; though we seldom get in touch or seek each other's company, except for rare family celebrations or calamities. I guess the reason for our lack of cohesion could be our fragmented and unsettled early life-style. With my father being in the Army, postings were all too frequent and the family had to relocate several times. Theo and I attended boarding schools, where terms were nine months long. This meant that for the best part of the year, we were away from family life - only spending the remaining three months in their company. It was hardly conducive to a close-knit family environment. Another possible excuse is that, less than a year after arriving in the UK, I joined the Merchant Navy, which meant again, I only saw the family briefly between voyages.

Then, a few months after we arrived in England, my father underwent surgery to remove much of his TB-diseased lungs. However, in spite of its debilitating effects, he seemed determined to increase the size of the family, a legacy I fear, from colonial times in India, where large families were the order of the day. In common with most of the indigenous populations of lesser-developed regions of the world, my ancestors believed it was vital to have numerous offspring as a kind of insurance/retirement policy. The rapid increase in our family meant that I never really got to know the four younger additions and soon, complete detachment came when I was called up for National Service. By then, the overcrowded conditions of a fourth floor council flat in North London persuaded me to drift further away. There was little or no feeling of belonging anywhere.

Few of us can boast a faultless memory, yet we casually commit vital information to it, in the forlorn hope that it will remain there. While important information like people's names, dental appointments, family birthdays, weddings anniversaries and such can easily escape our feeble memories, paradoxically, events from the distant past can often be clearly recalled at the snap of the fingers. I have discussed this strange characteristic with many of my contemporaries who also admit to this eccentricity. Thankfully, I am certainly no exception.

Behavioural scientists agree that, in general, our memory bank becomes particularly rich between the ages of ten and thirty, though exceptions are also common, depending on the degree and variety of notable experiences within one's life. Some however, may have little or no meaningful significance when memorised later.

Personally speaking, I suffer from an acute attack of embarrassment when questioned about details of my family's dates of birth, their ages or even my car registration number. On the other hand, I seem able to recall events in my early childhood with astonishing clarity - some significant, others quite meaningless. I would however, be quick to dismiss any notion of exceptional powers of recall, far from it! Psychoanalysts would say that we are more likely to remember the good things that happened to us in our lives, rather than the bad ones; I beg to differ! From my personal experience, people whose young lives were subject to strict parental control and who were placed in educational establishments with a culture of harsh discipline could be forgiven for saying that their childhood memories contained significantly more of the latter than the former.

Like many people of my generation, my short-term memory frequently fails me. While the passing of time may have also reduced my ability to recall certain life events, some indelible occurrences, locations and familiar characters, that influenced my early childhood, will remain with me for my entire life. Such flashbacks seem to occur during periods of solitude or whenever my memory has been refreshed by visual imagery, like news reports or travelogues with connections to the land of my birth. It is as if I were seeking some sort of comfort, in a perverse way, by invoking retrospective thoughts.

As the years pass I now find that all my aspirations have gradually melted away, leaving me with just thoughts of a misspent youth and so many squandered opportunities. However, to balance this, I do have the satisfaction of having experienced so many of the rich and diverse cultures of this incredible world in which we live.

Last Word

Thank you very much for reading this far. If you have found the book interesting and entertaining please be so kind as to recommend it to your family and friends and please leave a comment.

Thank you.

Printed in Great Britain
by Amazon